#Fishing Like a Girl

#Fishing Like a Girl

❧

From the 10,000 Islands and Beyond

Judy Weston

ISBN: 1517736765
ISBN 13: 9781517736767
Library of Congress Control Number: 2015916772
CreateSpace Independent Publishing Platform
North Charleston, South Carolina

CHAPTER 1

Beginnings

"HONEY, *HOW* DID that happen?"

I tried my best to untangle the fishing line that now encircled my entire body. *Yeah, how* did *this happen?* I thought, unable to respond. My predicament only worsened as I struggled to free myself from my monofilament captor. I had mistakenly cast my fishing line into a tree.

As I stood on the bow of our boat, I grew increasingly impatient for Chris to assist me. I grunted and groaned and yanked hard at the line, attempting to dislodge it. *Snap!* The tension from my tugging sent the line, weight, and hook hurling toward me with unrestraint. Somehow the flailing hook at the end of my line found the back of my pink tank top and latched on: now I had caught myself.

"Yeah, yeah. I know what you're thinking—I fish like a girl. Now can you *please* help me out here?" I was desperate. The sun's searing rays were baking me like a potato.

"Why don't you wear a bikini?" Chris asked for the umpteenth time. He untangled me as if he were taking lights off a Christmas tree.

"Stop asking me that!" I replied, annoyed. "Hurry up and unhook me!"

I can't be certain how I became a passionate fisherman—it just happened. My companion of several years—now my husband—lived and breathed the aquatic life. Naturally I took the plunge, and now I sometimes find myself in the middle of the wilderness, held hostage by my own wayward line. Fishing was a challenge that I was willing to attempt since I'm not much of a scrapbooker (I try) or interested in cooking (I gave up), and I am certainly not a preener (no way). I've tried to accept advice from caring girlfriends who give me pointers for fixing my hair or applying makeup, but every attempt has been unavailing. I do envy my friends who have the girl essentials down, but I'm better suited to challenging myself in other ways, such as hooking a redfish or maybe a spanish mackerel. Besides, I'm a fisherman, not a beauty-pageant contestant.

Once I'd been freed from my unruly line, Chris and I paused momentarily and began making plans for our next destination. "How about the Gulf?" he asked.

"Sounds good to me," I replied. I didn't care where we went, but I was happy there wouldn't be any trees around. But what Chris really wanted to do, I realized, was look for triple tail. I cringed. I had spoken too soon. I'm not a big fan of this fishing technique. You weave and swerve near crab traps to look for the elusive fish that looks like a gob of mud with fins. "Oh gosh!" I groaned. "Not the triple-tail tango." The method is like a dance: you glide on a tilted trajectory, swerving near the crab lines, careful not to harm them. The process just makes me dizzy. At my urging, we ended our search and sped away to more open water. I just don't have the patience for that drive-by kind of fishing.

Out on the water, I keep it all very simple. I usually wear shorts with pockets, a tank top, sandals, and sometimes earrings just for Chris, who scoffs at the sight and wonders why I bother when I'm out fishing. I'm not big on investing in a lot of gear since I don't need very much. I have my Outlaw custom rod and Penn reel, a strong line, a few swivels, a half-ounce weight, some two-aught hooks, leader line, and my husband, Chris. My entire tackle box could probably fit into the back pocket of my favorite blue jeans. Catching fish is less about gear and more about intuition and the ability to think like a fish. When I started out just a few years ago, I had neither. But this has been changing.

"Hey, Chris, there's the marker," I yelled over the roar of the engine. In the distance, a wooden stake jutting out of the water alert boaters that they are nearing the boundaries of the Everglades National Park that are spread out in the Gulf. Fish like structure, I have discovered, so we idled over a short distance from our target. Chris shut off the engine to determine which way the current and winds were going. Sometimes these two acts of nature conflict with each other, and the astute fisherman must discern the differences in order to successfully anchor. I noted the direction of the current and directed Chris as I knelt on the bow. "A little more to the right!" I yelled and tossed out the anchor at the perfect moment.

As the breeze picked up, I began to cast more to the side of the marker. Glancing skyward, I stuck my head in the clouds and got lost in a daydream. *Flip! Flop!* I was startled out of my thoughts by an odd noise. Looking toward the deck, I saw a fish! *Fish falling from the sky? What is this?* I adjusted my eyes and yelled to Chris, who was busy fishing. "Chris, something just jumped in our boat!"

"What?" he yelled back, never taking his eyes off his target.

"A *fish* just jumped in our boat," I replied loudly.

"What kind of fish?" he shouted, not even feigning interest.

"I don't know! Look at it, will you?" I rolled my eyes in frustration.

Chris turned his attention to my plea, and his eyes widened with excitement. "It's a pompano! Hurry up—change your bait and put on shrimp!" he bellowed. I didn't bother to ask why he was so thrilled about pompano. *OK, a pompano*, I thought. *It looks like a jack crevalle to me.* By this time Chris was in a fishing frenzy and wasted no time casting about. After the chaos, he managed to hook a few keepers.

"This is one of my favorite fish to eat," he said with a pompano-eating grin. "I like to cover the fillet in the crumbs of macadamia nuts. It's delicious!" he added with appreciative eyes.

The ride toward land felt brisk that day. The spray from the Gulf waters shot over the gunnels and hit my sunburned skin. Approaching land, I was entertained by a pair of determined osprey that plunged toward the water's surface with their talons at the ready, hoping to capture their prey. Nearby, leaping mullet caught my attention, and further to the south, dolphins spewed out breaths of air, culminating in a memorable Cirque du eau Soleil. I was grateful for the front-row seat.

"OK, we're heading for Fakahatchee Bay," Chris yelled. I gave the thumbs-up, still admiring the wildly winsome show.

The tide in the backcountry had lowered enough to expose some of the secrets hidden by higher waters. The leaves of the lower branches of the mangroves were lined with remnants of salt, looking like the rim of a margarita glass, while exposed insects hurried to seek shelter elsewhere. In the distance I could see the beaches come alive: hundreds of fiddler crabs scampered sideways, creating the illusion of a moving floor, while egrets stepped lively through the heavy, wet sands, gobbling up whatever they could at the water's edge. Opportunity had briefly exposed itself; in a few hours the protection of the waters would once again rise and cover it up.

After a few more stops, we called it a day and made our way down the idle zone of Port of the Islands. The lengthy ride gave us the chance to snack on chips and drink a few beers. We watched herons squabble over hunting grounds and observed a solitary alligator drift in the calm waters. We approached the dock slowly, and I took over the navigating.

"OK, I'll be right back with the truck," Chris said as he took off toward the parking lot. Once he backed the trailer in the water, I gripped the wheel, confident in my newly acquired boating skills. I cut through the calm waters as if through warm butter and drove the boat up on the trailer without a problem. A smattering of applause erupted from the fillet station, where a group of men admired my finesse with enthusiasm. I waved in acknowledgment. I was somewhat perplexed by their approval. I realize that fishing is still a male-dominated sport, but I felt in some way that I had just scored one for the girls.

CHAPTER 2

Full Moon

"TURN YOUR WHEEL the opposite way! No—turn the *other* way! Watch out! Go slow! Stop!" Chris's commands resonated loudly from the safety of the trees he was standing behind as I tightened my grip on the truck's steering wheel. I didn't know that learning to tow a boat on a trailer would be a lot like learning the salsa. Your thoughts are moving one way, and your partner—which happens to be a boat—is moving in another. Somehow the two movements are supposed to work together in effortless coordination. "Don't think about it too much," Chris kept advising.

"Let's take a ride down the street," Chris suggested as he seated himself on the passenger side. "Just take your turns wide." I mustered up the courage, nodded my head, and turned onto the main road. I would say it went fairly well—if you disregard the fact that I tipped over a trash can and hit a few curbs. "OK, you got this," Chris said. "Most girls can't or won't pull a trailer, but you can!" (I think that comment was an attempt at flattery.) "Now we can take the camper and the boat to Chokoloskee!" And the next weekend we were packing our camper and boat for a three-day fishing trip.

On the morning of our departure, I had a bad case of pull-the-boat jitters and did my best to conceal it by pumping up my own morale. We departed and made our way toward Tamiami Trail under a cloudless sky. I was following Chris, who was pulling the camper. I towed our Pathfinder 24. "Don't think about it too much," I grumbled to myself as I pulled our boat along the bumpy road. It wouldn't have been so bad if the Pathfinder wasn't loaded with embellishments such as a Yamaha engine that stuck out like the tail of a

Tennessee Walker and a T-top that hovered high like a Macy's parade balloon. This was becoming a little more than I had bargained for.

The roads leading to Chokoloskee Island are fairly straight. There are no wild curves (unless you factor in the road construction), and so far my maiden voyage was going well, excluding the part when Chris missed his turn and I eagerly followed. He left the parking lot unscathed, while I resembled a steel ball in an arcade pinball machine, pinging and dinging against scuffed curbs through the lot's narrow lanes and tight turns. All eyes were on me as I rolled through, smiling as my emergency lights flashed on and off. My newfound moxie stayed strong, and after I bumped the last curb, my fiberglass partner and I rolled out of there and caught up with Chris.

The landscape turned to grassy rivers where egrets and hawks scoured the fields for food against a panoramic view of forever. Tiny tributaries that looked like veins in a hand stretched toward an infinite horizon, disturbed only by the light breeze that skirted its murky surface. We arrived at the threshold of a vibrant world of exotic foliage and mystical beasts that do their best to ignore the rambling vehicles that threaten to disturb their home. I'm always humbled by its innocent grandeur and vow to do my best to be respectful.

That evening at a café in Everglades City, we pored over charts that were shellacked onto the table where we shared a hot bowl of chili. "Here we are, and here is Lostmans River," Chris said, pointing with a fork. My eyes widened at all the meticulously penned small inlets and tributaries that offered a bird's-eye view of the area. After wiping off a few spills of hot sauce from the map, we settled on a few possibilities. It all depended on the mood of the sea and its tides, so finalizing our plans would have to wait for the morning. Weather forecasters can provide some insight into conditions, but I have found that Mother Nature doesn't always follow those predictions.

Looking toward the morning sky as I walked briskly to the dock, I noticed the faint remnants of a celestial object, appearing strangely arcane as it made its descent into the distant horizon. This lunar vision of night was being slowly extinguished by the Gulf of Mexico. Some fishermen boast that the fishing will be excellent during the full moon, while others contend that the brilliance of this orb in darkness allows the fish to feed in its illumination, leaving them uninterested in the breakfast offerings of the early fishermen. I know that the moon rules the tides, but the sun has always been my guide, and—full moon or not—I will always hook a fish sometime during the day.

We opted to head to the Gulf of Mexico, where the winds were light and the water's surface was calm. After nearly an hour, we approached our destination. "There it is, Lostmans River!" Chris exclaimed as his endearing eyes grew wide. It was as if he were seeing an old friend for the first time in many years. "This could get scary," he warned as he slowed the boat down.

"What do you mean, *scary*?" I inquired, shocked at this new description for the river.

"Shallow waters, that's what I mean." We crept along like a cat stalking its prey, slowly idling to the river's entrance, where deeper water awaited. "Whew, that was nuts!" Chris sighed as he relaxed back into his chair.

Scanning the banks for any inkling of fish, Chris settled on the textured banks that stretched southward, where the Gulf waters and the river meet. "I've caught sheepshead, snapper, and snook along this bank," Chris said. "Let's anchor up and see what's here," he added with an enthusiastic grin.

I sat on the gunnels with my rod and checked the drag on my line. When you check the drag, you tug on the fishing line to check how easily the line moves. The thin monofilament should be loose enough to allow a big fish to run but tight enough so that it won't spool you—taking your bait and your entire line, too. I whispered to myself, "Spool me once, shame on me. Spool me twice, shame on me again!" and stood up ready for the fight.

Chris was reeling in mangrove snapper. The legal keeping size of this fish is ten inches from its nose to the fork of the tail, but we decided to increase that length to eleven inches to decrease the number for us to harvest. There were plenty of ten inchers, but we felt it wasn't necessary to keep them. I reeled in a nice-sized snapper. Chris yelled over, "You can put that one in the cooler!" and went back to what he was doing. I was reluctant to place this lively fish into an icy tomb, so I headed toward the live well. I figured fish purgatory was better than the cooler and that if I could keep it alive, there could be a chance that it would be released back into the sea. Placing it in the live well meant that I could have a change of heart, something that happens more times than not.

Chris set his sights on a bank with a deep hole adjacent to it. "There could be some big fish here," he said with that excitement I've come to know. It wasn't long after anchoring that he hooked a large redfish. The fish took some time to get on board, but once we did it, celebratory yells filled the air. Chris took his catch and walked to the cooler, and I headed for the bow to get in a few more casts before we pulled anchor and called it a day. "We'll take the Wilderness Waterway back to camp," Chris said.

On our way back, we passed through various bays and tributaries, marveling at this magnum opus of nature while appreciating the day's catch. Chris slowed the boat down while approaching Alligator Creek, where sun-bleached branches tapped at the surface of the ebony waters. The sun had slipped behind gray clouds, muting the colors of the creek, hushing the vibrant greens, and quieting the stark contrast of the bright sunlight. As we idled through this utopian estuary, the sound of water gently washing over the exposed roots of the mangrove nearly lulled me to sleep. "OK, let's get ready to take off," Chris said, jarring me from my restful posture.

Approaching the dock near our campsite, we were greeted by friendly anglers. "Catch any fish?" asked a tall man with sandy-brown hair and sunburned cheeks.

"Sure did!" Chris exclaimed. "I got a nice red." He reached into the cooler and proudly lifted the chilled fish toward their covetous eyes.

"Nice!" they yelled in unison, nodding their sweaty heads. After the brief encounter, I turned toward our boat and heard an unusual sound. I glanced in the direction of the disturbance and watched as the man with the sunburned cheeks toss a live fish on the fillet board and started hacking into it with an electric knife. The mechanical blades dug deep into the fish's flesh. Its mouth opened and shut several times and then went still. I couldn't believe this was happening. *Doesn't he care? Doesn't he respect the fish? Why doesn't he have the decency to at least let it die on ice before cutting into it?*

This draconian method went on for several minutes. Fish after flailing fish was tossed up with little regard, and metal blades sliced quickly into the flesh by the hands of this friendly man whom I had just had the pleasure of exchanging words with. I felt awful for the fish, whose carcasses were being fed to the hungry pelicans that bobbed up and down at the edge of the dock. I wanted badly to say something, but I stopped myself. I realized that if I told him he was wrong, he'd probably point out that I use live bait. What's the difference, after all? I stick a sharp hook through the belly of a live shrimp and pierce the skulls of young fish fingerlings all day with no problem. I was sure there was a difference, but I wasn't sure what that difference was.

Walking away from the scene, I approached our camper, opened the door, and walked into the cool air. I took off my sunglasses and reached for a drink from the refrigerator, which hummed a lonesome sound. I passed by our bay window and glanced out toward the weathered dock. Standing tall against a brilliant blue sky, the sunburned man with sandy-brown hair continued to carve the flailing fish like a Thanksgiving Day turkey as brown pelicans bobbed at the dock's edge, hoping for something.

CHAPTER 3

— ❧ —

Frayed Line, Fraid Not

"Chris, there's a ghost floating in the water!" I said jokingly, noticing the pallid presence of a bonnethead shark. Its motion seemed sublime, and its spooky demeanor remained unchanged even after I cast a line in its direction. Unfazed by the minor disturbance, the pale creature continued to haunt me for several minutes before vanishing into the copper-colored waters of West Pass River. I couldn't help but to be momentarily hypnotized by the image of the strange-looking visitor and missed a bite because of it. "Damn, I missed." I was frustrated by my lack of concentration. It can be really easy to lose focus in that environment, ghost or no ghost.

Chris and I managed to go through a lot of shrimp in a short amount of time, and we agreed that we should seek out more bait. "We have enough shrimp to try a few more spots," Chris said, and we pulled anchor. I have discovered that finding fish entails a great deal of idling around. Currents, the shallows, points on a bank, tides, the phase of the moon, coves, deep holes, and a little luck are just a few of the many details that are important to finding the kind of fish you are looking for. "Look over there at that point." Chris motioned as we crept to the bank that held promise and hope-fully a fish worthy of keeping. "I've caught reds, snook, and sheepshead in this area," he said with absolute confidence as he began to drop the anchor.

True to his prediction, I got a big tug, and it was game on. In an instant everything went silent. I focused all of my senses on the feel of the fish. *Keep the line tight, tip up, breathe, and don't panic!* I silently coached myself as the power of the fish began to confuse me.

"Play the fish!" Chris screamed as a large redfish appeared at the surface. "Play it—don't horse it!" At that point I was too busy to try to decipher what *play it* and *horse it* meant.

"Get the net *now*!" I yelled through clenched teeth. My arms began to tremble. Chris hurried over, and just as he began to dip the net into the water to scoop up my prize, *tink*! The line broke. I lost it!

Somewhere in the depths of West Pass, there's a big redfish swimming around with a permanently pierced mouth. *I hope it'll be OK*, I thought sullenly. Chris walked over and quietly reminded me of the old saying "Frayed line, fraid not." He could tell by the course texture of what was left of my line that it had seen better days.

After losing a big fish, there is a certain kind of reflection that takes place. Chris went back to the bow, picked up his rod, and continued fishing. I sat sulking while my broken line fluttered in the afternoon breeze. When your line becomes frayed by the scraping of rocks, oysters, and other debris, you better change it out, or you'll end up losing your fish, as I have so painfully found out. With steely resolve I decided to end my sulking and start rigging. *I'm not going to make it up to myself if I don't get back up and start again*, I thought as the jumping mullet softly splashed in the background.

Chris is known for having an enterprising spirit, and he decided to take the boat in a different direction. "What are you doing?" I asked, puzzled by our sudden change of direction. "Why aren't we heading toward Tiger Key?"

"Let's try a new area—something different for a change," he said, scanning the horizon for potential points of interest.

"I'd *prefer* places that we've fished before. Can we go back there?" I said, pointing toward a familiar setting.

Chris promptly rebuffed my suggestion and continued on. "C'mon, honey, it's an *adventure*," he said in his charming way. His hair blew wildly in the wind. My paltry protest had fallen on deaf ears, and I quickly abandoned any hope of going back toward our accustomed locations. I decided to be a better sport about the whole thing. This was his day out on the water, and I wanted him to enjoy himself.

"This looks kinda good," Chris said. He remarked on how the current seemed to be hitting the tip just right and said something about water movement sweeping around the corner. Chris has an uncanny knack for finding reliable fishing areas, so I wasn't surprised when I started reeling in fighting jacks and beefy snappers.

"Hey—we should mark this spot on the GPS," Chris happily uttered after landing a few nice catches himself. When you have moving water that rushes against a point, you are almost guaranteed good fishing. A current carries fish like a running back carries a ball, although it's uncertain, as with any attempt, if you will come up with a winning catch.

Sundown was not far off, and at my urging we returned to familiar locations. We anchored up, and before casting I checked my line for any deficiencies and found none. I confidently tossed out a cast and watched it form a perfect arc in the sky and then land inches from the roots of a mangrove tree.

"Nice cast, honey," Chris said, admiring my precision. Without warning, my line pulled with great force. I pulled tight and used a steady hand as I reeled in.

"Get the net," I yelled, grimacing. "It's a red!" I began talking to myself, almost chanting: "Please don't break; please, line, don't break." The fish inched closer to the gunnels as I held my tip up and kept the line tight. "Hurry!" I feared I would lose the fish at any minute. Chris quickly dipped the net into the darkness and scooped up my prize.

"Nice fish," he said. "And it's a keeper!" Chris put the net down and placed the fish in the live well. He then turned around, reached in the cooler, and popped the top on a cold beer. "You want the first drink?" he said, smiling.

"Sure do!" I stretched my hand out to grab the can as I whispered toward the sky, thanking God for the gift of fish and cold beer.

It was time to head back to the ramp, and I agreed to drive the boat up onto the trailer. I watched Chris slowly back the truck into the water and step out, waving me in. With the confidence of an NFL special teams player, I easily sliced the water and drove up through the trailer guide poles, which resemble uprights, and clicked into place. My first attempt at trying to trailer the boat, I must say, wasn't so flawless. I came in too fast, panicked, and drove the boat into the ramp horizontally! The men who were around started jumping around, Chris was yelling, and I was mortified. Thankfully, with help, we saved the boat from crashing directly into the concrete ramp. It wasn't a pretty sight, but Chris took it all in stride.

I could hear the sound of dripping water as Chris pulled the boat over so we could prepare for travel. Several men walked over, and one congenially commented, "We watched you pull that boat right up. You're pretty good for a girl!"

"Oh, thanks," I replied, shrugging off the perceived compliment.

"Yeah, and she keeps reeling them in, too!" Chris added.

"What did you catch?" This is a question fishermen ask each other often; it's pretty standard.

"Oh, snapper, mackerel, and a *real* nice red," Chris said coyly, as he tightened the last strap on the back of the boat.

"Where did you get the red?" they pressed.

"Well, it was kind of around West Pass," Chris responded, intentionally vague. The fishermen didn't press any further and went back to filleting their fish. They were fully aware that we were not about to give up a prime location.

Wet and tired, we got in the truck and headed for home. "Why do you think those guys were so impressed with my boating?" I asked as we drove over the Goodland Bridge. "Every time I drive the boat up, there always seems to be a crowd of guys eyeing me as if I were part of some sort of show!" I laughed.

"I guess they think it's pretty cool that you can do that," he said.

"Drive a boat up on a trailer?" I responded, perplexed by the notion.

"Well, you're a *girl!*" he said with a wink and a smile.

"Good grief!" I replied, as the last few boats idled near Coon Key Marina, waiting for their turn at the ramp.

CHAPTER 4

—— ✿ ——

White Turtle

THE FORECAST HADN'T mentioned any downpours, yet there on the horizon off White Horse Key were the makings of a beastly storm. "That doesn't look so good," I said to Chris as he disembarked from the boat and onto the shore, where a cluster of mangroves swayed like dancers on a sandy stage. This solitary beacon of delicious serenity belied the ominous backdrop that inched nearer with each gust of the wind, and I wondered what we would do.

"I'll throw here," he gestured, and readied his cast net for potential bait. I hadn't attempted any net throwing yet, but I was intently observing and made mental notes on the techniques Chris was using. *Clench the weights of the net with your teeth, hold the throwing arm straight, scan the surface of water looking for any rippling, bend, twist, and throw!* This is the method that he learned as a young boy and still continues to use.

After several attempts, the only things he was catching in the net were mud, sticks, and leaves. "Well, maybe we'll try later. The tide is going out anyway." He began to fold up the once-white mesh that was now tinged brown. "We'll head east and hopefully lose that storm," he said, glancing toward the west, and we set our sights toward the backcountry. A deep appreciation for the Ten Thousand Islands swept over me as the blurry details of the absinthe vista hurried by. There are countless areas for fishing; you just have to discover the right spot. And that requires a fisherman's astute analysis. Fortunately for me, Chris is an exceptional thinker. I swear, if you cut his wrist, he would bleed brackish water.

Our boat slowed, and we drifted with the current to assess its direction. After much thought, we anchored near an area where the current skirted the hem of the bank. "This looks good," Chris said. He baited his line and took a cast. My excitement and competitive spirit got the best of me, and I overzealously cast into a tree.

"Ugh!" I groaned, and I freed my line with one strong tug. My next cast flew with promise, sank, and quickly got caught on a rock. "That's it—I want to go home," I protested. Chris was strangely silent during my outburst and kept fishing, ignoring me completely. I didn't *really* want to go home; what I wanted was a fish on my line, not on a rock or a tree!

"Now pay attention and watch how *not* to get caught on the rocks," he caringly spoke. I watched as he tossed his line out and gently raised his tip real easy. "If you slowly raise your tip, it'll hop right over those rocks."

I calmed myself down and decided to give Chris's method a chance. Feeling optimistic, I tossed out my line and waited for it to sink. I gently lifted the tip and reeled slowly. "Hey, I felt the hook and my sinker go over the rock!" I yelled. On my next gentle reel, I got a big tug and, to my surprise, landed a gag grouper.

"See? I told you it would work!" he said, beaming with pride. A rocky bottom can be challenging, but it's a great place to find fish that use the structure as a refuge. We released the undersized grouper, and I continued to practice my newfound technique while Chris reeled in several sizeable sheepshead.

After great success with that location, we decided to pull anchor and head for one of our favorite areas, near Fakahatchee Bay. After a short ride, we pulled up to a cluster of gnarly branches that scratched the surface of the water. "This is an excellent area for fish," Chris commented. The tides were rolling strong, and after a few attempts at anchoring, we finally caught. Anchoring in strong currents can be challenging due to the strength of the water grabbing your anchor as it floats toward the bottom. It might seem weighty, but it doesn't stand a chance against a mighty current. Sometimes it will hit the bottom and just plow along, unable to grasp anything.

The sky above turned milky, but it kept the sun's hot rays at bay, and gentle winds provided some protection from the mosquitoes. We began casting in earnest, starting slow and then picking up the pace as we hooked snapper and several sheepshead.

My hunger pangs had begun to be too much of a distraction, and I paused long enough to have a seat and look out upon the beauty of the bay area. It was during this lull that I observed something so unique, so oddly aberrant, that I wasn't sure what to do or say. I turned toward Chris and noticed he had a similar look of befuddlement. "Did you see that? It was a white turtle—an albino turtle!" I yelled with astonishment.

"Yeah, I believe you're right," Chris replied. I sat for a moment to try to process what I had just witnessed. *Did I really see a white turtle?* Chris had caught a glimpse, too, but the vision continued to bewilder me. *Whom can I tell? Who would care as much as I? Would anyone believe it?*

After the brief encounter, I tossed out a few lines, trying my best to not think about the rare sighting and concentrate on my backhand throw. The bite slowed with the tide, and it was off to somewhere else. There was no need to stick around when there were plenty of choices: they don't call it the Ten Thousand Islands for nothing. We zipped through the bay, searching the landscape for clues that would lead us to the biting fish.

Chris settled on an area that wasn't far off the beaten path. As we anchored, a swooshing sound startled us. "Oh gosh, it's a pelican," I said, relieved it wasn't something malfunctioning on our boat. Just to our port side, a large pelican with faded feathering bobbed contently, casting its brown eyes in our direction. At first its presence wasn't a bother; then I understood what its motive was. I cast my line and began pulling in my catch, and the pelican dove quickly toward the fish, attempting to steal it from my line. I reeled in quickly, avoiding the brown bandit's gallant effort.

"Shoo," I said toward the bird that was still shaking off the water from its shrewd attempt. "Chris, it won't go away." I stopped casting and pondered the problematic state of affairs. If I cast out and the pelican was successful at capturing my fish, it would be placed in serious peril. It would swallow not only the fish, but the hook and line, too. Pausing momentarily, I recalled a horrid sight we'd once witnessed while passing one of the markers that alert boaters to the park boundaries. Idling by, we noticed a dead pelican rotting in the wind, hanging upside down. Apparently it had been trapped by an errant fishing line. Hundreds of birds perch there, and I'd never witnessed such a thing before. I had to cover my eyes. Growing increasingly despondent over the abhorrent vision, I pleaded for Chris to hurry by. We had no way to rescue the bird from its entrapment to offer its body a more suitable final resting place. We continued on in silence. Chris and I are diligent at recovering our lines and disposing of them properly, and that scene—which still haunts me today—is a ghastly reminder of what can go wrong.

"We should call this place Pesky Pelican Point," Chris joked, pulling up anchor to find another place. We puttered to an adjacent island, and just before we dropped anchor, *poof*—the pelican reappeared. *It looks like we're stuck with this pelican like gum on a shoe*, I thought.

"Well, let's go. This is no good," Chris said, and I agreed. I knew we weren't going to attempt any more fishing in the area—not with that crafty hunter near. Pulling the anchor once again, we began our departure slowly and picked up speed as we headed for Coon Key. The brown pelican with the tucked chin innocently bobbed with the rhythm of the waves and eventually disappeared from view.

As we approached the ramp, we noticed a flurry of activity at the fillet station. "They must have a lot of fish," I said in wonderment. We loaded up the boat, and Chris went for a closer look. He came back to tell me that they had harvested a ton of whiting fish. I was skeptical at their bounty and asked Chris why they had kept so many. "I don't really know," he said. "Maybe there's no limit on that particular fish," he continued, hopping into the truck.

Driving off, I glanced back through the rearview mirror, where I could see men with busy hands rummaging near the fillet station while hungry birds swooped around, hoping for an easy meal. The parting scene reminded me something I had read in a flyer provided by an Everglades Park ranger. It read, "Limit your take don't take your limit." *Hmm, maybe I'll nail a sign on the railing that reads just that*, I thought.

CHAPTER 5

— ❧ —

Lightning Strikes

MOST ARDENT ANGLERS know that patience is one of the absolute greatest attributes one can possess. It's an accoutrement you won't find in the aisles of your local sporting goods store, and it's not something you can borrow. It's a process of discovery and is often acquired through long hours on the water when the fish aren't biting. Composure would serve me well, but that character component has continued to elude me. This glaring hindrance has been a big problem for my angler ambitions and persistently nags my fishing arm while I cast and come up empty.

"Honey, you have to leave your line *in* for a few minutes if you want a bite," my husband calmly repeated, lifting his rod up with yet another flipping fish. I blankly stared in his direction, momentarily watching his angling finesse and growing increasingly envious. "Look, honey, keep your line tight and be patient," he calmly continued, and he wrangled in another weighty snapper.

While I continued making attempts to cast correctly, Chris made the decision to take a time out and head for Tiger Key. "We can get some better bait on Tiger Key," he said assuredly. We made our way west for several curvy miles, and as the sight of Tiger Key came into view, Chris pulled back on the throttle. The nearing shoreline seemed to come alive as dozens of red crabs hurried sideways to find cover from our impending approach. As we crept closer, the hushed environment offered a sense of tranquility that was occasionally interrupted by the soft sounds of white-washed seashells clinking and clanking with every gentle push from the incoming tide.

Our boat hit the sand with a thunk that jarred me loose from a daydream and my cushioned seat. Chris opened the hatch and reached for his casting net, stepped into his sandals, and slid off the gunnels and into the tepid waters. "Make sure the anchor is secure," he said. His footsteps left deep impressions in the moistened sand that were promptly filled in by the surging sea.

"You'll catch bigger fish with bigger bait," Chris reminded me. He hurled the white mesh into the air, and it quickly fell with a swish. "Do you think I got any?" Chris slowly tugged his net through the soupy water.

"Sure!" I yelled back. As his net neared the shore, a hint of shimmering silver appeared.

"Wow, look at this!" Chris exclaimed. He began emptying the net onto the sand and yelled for me to come over with the bait bucket I haphazardly held in my hand. I scrambled to scoop up the sizeable bait fish that arched, flipped, leaped, and rolled their way toward the water, hoping to escape my human hands. Some died on the spot, and some lay motionless, stunned by their predicament. Fish don't scream, but they exhibit fear: it's in their eyes, and that day I felt as if I could see it. I weighed out my approach with Chris concerning this epiphany and decided to set aside the troubling thoughts. I looked away as I scooped up the last of the wiggling fish. "OK, we have enough!" Chris said, shaking me out of my bewilderment.

The ride up river was refreshingly fun. The coolness of the air and the partly cloudy sky provided relief from the idle air on Tiger Key, and I threw my head back to capitalize on the rushing wind. "Here's the place I wanted to take you," Chris said, stopping the boat and instructing me to throw the anchor out. "Toss it out quickly, and tie her off," he barked, and I hurriedly made figure eights around the steely cleat. I took the bow and he took the stern, and it wasn't long before the first reel screamer happened. *Wheeeeezzzz!* "Honey, get the net! I got a big one!"

It appeared that he had Moby Dick on the other end, considering the bend in his rod. "Big fish!" he breathlessly whispered, struggling to hold on. The line stalled, forcing Chris to wait. "I think it's a grouper," Chris said, huffing and puffing. Groupers are notorious for using their girth to seat themselves on the bottom and wait as the annoying line continues to tug at their lip.

Big and smart, they usually have their way with your flimsy monofilament and wait for it to snap. Another tactic the fish has up its crafty fin is to seek refuge in the mangroves that thrive along the banks. Once a fish is secure in the shadows, a fisherman can do little to coax it from the safety of the strong, interwoven roots.

Slow and steady, Chris stayed the course and dislodged the creature from the bottom. A shimmering of gold flickered as the fish surfaced and then sank, still struggling for its freedom. "Ugh!" Chris groaned. "It's a jewfish!" A jewfish, also known as a Goliath Grouper, is a protected species and has a rounded tail, I found out. "We can't keep it. It's off-limits. I've got to get it off the hook fast." He reached down and attempted to dislodge the hook that was embedded perfectly in its massive lip.

"We have to bring it on board. I don't want to hurt it," he said, and his long arms dipped into the darkness. Lifting this hefty grouper, I soon discovered, would be the equivalent of hoisting a hippo over your head—these fish are heavy! "One, two, three, *up!*" Chris shouted. We worked as a team, and with one more yank, the beast was on deck. Even the smaller goliath groupers such as this one are weighty and require great care when dislodging the hook.

Every inch of this fish was full of life, and its gills rapidly opened and closed like an accordion. Its base color had an amber wash with flecks of gold that created the illusion of a treasure unearthed. Chris was working as fast as he could, but this fish knew how to throw its weight around. I grabbed a towel, threw it over its squirming body, and lay on it just enough to keep it still. I now had a full-body press, albiet gentle, on a protected species.

"Chris, how much *longer?*" I asked as nonchalantly as I could. I felt the pounding of its heart against mine, and I was unable to distinguish whose was beating harder. With a few more careful twists, Chris dislodged the hook. He lifted the fish and placed it with care into the river, where it sank and swam down, leaving a wake at the surface and distorting my reflection with every ripple.

The sky had changed to ashen gray, and I wondered where the sun's rays had gone so quickly. A distant swooshing noise crept closer, and I realized what it was. "Chris, look!" I yelled, pointing toward a wall of wicked rain. The stealthy storm turned our way and threatened to overwhelm us.

"Pull anchor *now!*" Chris yelled to me. I had enough time to put my rain gear on and pull anchor as the storm stalled. Chris pushed the throttle forward, and I grabbed the metal pole of the T-top for stability. As we raced off, a bright light flashed, followed by a thunderous crack and boom as a large bolt of lightning struck near. I screamed out in terror and fell backward from the surge of electricity that raced through my veins, rattling every bone in my body. I trembled from the shock.

"Chris I just got hit by lightning!" I whimpered, still trying to determine if I was OK.

"What do you mean? Are you OK?" Chris asked with deep concern.

"I…I…I think so," I replied, still shivering from the experience.

"I don't think it hit you directly. You probably got some residual static electricity," he calmly told me.

Whatever it was, I considered myself lucky. I rubbed my arms, trying to provide comfort to my shaken senses.

"Well," Chris said matter-of-factly, "that's the way to the ramp." He pointed toward the deluge that had now intensified. Resignation swept over us hard, but we were undeterred. "I'm going to run through. Hold on!" he yelled, pushing the throttle forward and heading directly into the heart of Mother Nature's fury. There was no turning back.

Pow! Bang! Boom! Rrrrip! The sky's symphony reached its crescendo as the tempest raged on. I attempted to shield myself from the hard rain that was falling sideways, piercing my face. Through stinging eyes I glanced toward Chris. He was standing tall, resembling King Neptune as he drove on undaunted by the harrowing uncertainties that were before us, hidden by the blinding downpour.

"Can we slow down, for God's sake!" I yelled.

"We can't. We got to keep it on a plane—we're in the shallows!" he yelled back. The engine whined on.

Oh God, we're going to crash into some mangroves, I thought. *I can't see anything!* Nature's sound effects continued to fill the air as Chris zigged and zagged, confidently navigating the boat even though the sky and the water had melded together, creating the illusion of suspended animation. "How much longer?" I implored, but I received no answer.

By now I had grown numb to the possibility that this could end badly. "Chris, *how long?*" I asked again.

"Right around the corner," he yelled back, never taking his hazel eyes off the horizon. We approached the ramp as the rain started to slow, giving us enough time to load the boat before the next onslaught. I glanced back toward the direction we had just come from and saw the blackened sky light up with multiple lightning bolts that scratched the clouds.

"Let's hurry. It's heading this way," I said as calmly as I could.

Once in the warmth of our truck, I peeled off my jacket and tossed it in the backseat, and we made our way over the Goodland Bridge. In the distance a faint shade of blue opened up in the sky in the direction of our home. "Hey—look, Chris. Blue sky!" I said. A faint smile crossed my face. I knew it wouldn't be long before I could get some dry clothes on and greet my dogs, who were probably patiently waiting and wagging their tails, anticipating our return.

CHAPTER 6

— ❧ —

A Shark and a Boat

Standing on a solitary shoreline in ankIe-deep water, I helplessly watched my husband disappear into the turbulent waters of West Pass Bay, and I had to laugh. *Is this really happening?* Fear and terror have a strange way of distorting your reality, and mine had reached an epic level, which showed itself in fits of uncontrollable laughter. Trying to humor myself, I came up with a story that even Carl Hiaasen could be proud of: *Wife left alone on a desolate shoreline somewhere in the Ten Thousand Islands while husband swims after their boat that got away. Boat and husband disappear in shark-infested waters, and wife stands alone without food, water, telephone, and bug spray. The sun begins to fade into the Gulf of Mexico.* Unfortunately for me, the sun was fading, and my humorous musings were short-lived. This was not fiction; this was real. I *was* standing on a shoreline alone, and my husband really *had* disappeared from sight in shark-infested waters. And the boat was gone, too.

There was nothing inauspicious at all about our morning. Our day began as it usually does, letting the dogs out, making coffee, and preparing lunches. I went about my tasks happily, and Chris was busy packing coolers, rods, and other necessities for our fishing trip. We launched our boat from Coon Key and idled along, planning our target areas while embracing the crisp autumn air. "Hey, the Gulf is smooth. Let's head out to one of those markers," Chris said. I nodded in approval, and we made our way west.

We anchored easily, and I began the task of baiting my hook. I was using shrimp and thought nothing of the storm clouds that were far off to the north. "I'll cast from the bow," I mentioned to Chris.

"OK, I'll take the stern," he said, and off he went with his rod in tow. I was getting fish on the line, but they were small and mostly jacks.

"Nothing but jacks up here," I yelled back to Chris.

"Keep trying!" he yelled back. *OK, one more cast over to the south*, I thought, and I let my line fly. The bite was nothing unusual, and as I began reeling in, I walked closer to the bow and hung my toes over to get a better look. I continued reeling in slowly, watching my distorted reflection morphing into strange shapes to pass the time. And then I felt another tug. *Huh, what was that?* I remember thinking just before a large shadowy figure emerged from the depths.

I had no time to do anything. The bull shark fiercely shattered the surface of the water with its mouth wide open, trying to sink its teeth into me and my fish. How can anyone prepare for such a shocking turn of events? One minute I was relaxing while fishing in the Gulf of Mexico, and the next minute I found myself staring down into the jaws of a big shark that was about ready to pull me down into a watery grave. It didn't make sense. In a blur of gray, the shark made a last-minute turn away from me and splashed downward into the sea. I fell back onto the bow. My mind was aware of what happened, but I was having trouble processing it.

"What's going on?" Chris asked, alarmed by the sudden splashing.

"A shark just jumped out at me!" I said, trying hard to seem composed. I was all right, but I sure didn't feel like I was.

"Oh, it was probably going for your fish," Chris said, dismissing the event.

I stayed away from the bow and made a mental note for next time: when fishing off the bow, keep arms and legs away from the edge.

"We'll hit the backcountry now," Chris said. "Fishing has slowed here anyway." We headed out to West Pass to do some snapper fishing, even though it had already started to get late. Our favorite spot was really happening. We were hooking large mangrove snapper, but we got low on shrimp just as the action got better. "Let's head over to Tiger Key and get some bait. We still have time," Chris said, excited about the good fishing. We had spent most of the day pulling in small fish, and now our luck had changed.

The incoming tide was rolling nicely, and we had no trouble making the curve to get up on the shore of Tiger Key. "Let's make this quick," Chris said, and he dropped the shallow anchor down. Chris took the cast net to the south side of the island, and I wandered around, looking for shells.

I glanced over at the boat and noticed something peculiar. *Why is the boat sideways?* "Hey Chris, the boat looks funny. It doesn't look right," I yelled, running toward him.

"Oh God," he said with annoyance. "It looks like I'm going for a swim."

"A swim? What do you mean, a swim?" I asked nervously.

"The tide is coming in too fast, and the shallow anchor didn't hold," he said. He started taking off his T-shirt and walking toward the water.

"Hurry up!" I urged. I could tell the tide had picked up, and it seemed as if Chris was moving in slow motion. I was all amped up and about ready to jump in myself.

"Stay here," he said sternly. "I'll be right back."

At first it seemed like we would be OK, but each time Chris would get near the boat, it floated just outside of his grasp, almost as if it was toying with him. The boat continued to drift serenely out into the open bay, with Chris struggling to catch up to it. I ran up to the edge of the water, about to jump in and go after Chris, and I stopped. *I can't swim that well. This is not a good idea.* I started running up and down the bank, straining to see something, anything. *Is that him?* I could hear splashing off in the distance. *Oh God, did a shark get him? These* are *shark-infested waters. He has no weapons.* Panic set in. *Is this how it will end?* I recall thinking. I fell to my knees.

I pleaded my case to God. I screamed my screams, prayed my prayer, said my say, and cried my cry. There was nothing left for me to do but brace myself for whatever came next. I stood up and wiped the sand away from my knees, faced the bay, and waited. I stared out into the horizon, ignoring its beauty and looking for clues. Then I heard in the distance the sound of a horn. *Chris?* The unmistakable sound of an engine rumbled near, and then Chris, driving our Pathfinder, sped around the corner. I jumped up and down in a euphoric haze.

"I got the boat back!" he said as he pulled up, laughing. And then he leaned over and vomited off the side. We pulled away from the shore and headed back to the ramp. Fishing for the day was officially over, and I wrapped myself in a blanket, held onto my husband, and watched the blue sky fade to a dusky orange and red. Carl Hiaasen could not have penned it better.

CHAPTER 7

A Place Called Flamingo

In South Florida we have the luxury of choosing between several very different bodies of water to fish—the Gulf of Mexico, the Ten Thousand Islands, and Lake Okeechobee, to name a few. Chris kept talking about Flamingo, one of the many fishing destinations located in Everglades National Park. He touted it as one of his favorite areas, and he wanted to take me there. "You'll love it there, honey," he assured me. "It'll be fun."

"OK, let's go," I replied, without giving it much thought.

We packed up the camper and the boat and prepared ourselves for several days of adventure. Heading south on US 41, aka Tamiami Trail, we encountered billboards showing happy people and eye-catching landmarks that can easily lure you in. There's the Skunk Ape Research Center, Clyde Butcher's gallery that houses his impressive images of the Everglades, Joanie's Blue Crab Café, the smallest post office in the United States, and the Miccosukee Indian village, with its lively shops and shows. In addition to that, there are multiple airboat ride offerings that dot the landscape, enticing you with old-fashioned marketing techniques. Driving this fairly straight road still has its hazards, though. You have to be really careful not to run over the tourists who nonchalantly walk across the road to snap a few photos of sunbathing alligators.

With Chris pulling the camper and me towing the boat, the time trudged along. We were taking our time to ensure safety, and it made the journey much more pleasurable. "OK, honey, we're going to make the turn up here in Florida City, and it won't be much longer."

"Great!" I replied over my speakerphone, and I adjusted myself in my Silverado. We followed the signs that led to Everglades National Park, and upon our arrival we were greeted by a red flashing sign warning us that the mosquito level was seriously high. *Hmm, that shouldn't be a big deal—we brought spray*, I thought, and I continued toward the welcoming window, where I was ready to smile at the attendant and pay the entry fee. Chris approached first, paused at the window, and called me.

"There's nobody here," he said, "but there's a sign that says we could come on in."

Hmm…this is strange. Isn't this a national park? I thought. Chris went on through, and I crept up to the window where the crinkled handwritten sign dangled from a small piece of tape.

"Okaaay, this is different," I whispered. I scratched my arm where a welt was now forming, created by the bite of a mosquito that had stealthily zipped through my half-cracked window.

As we ambled along the two-lane road, the landscape continued to morph into something that was vastly different from our last few hours of driving. Gone were all the colorful billboards with fierce-looking alligators and signs depicting airboat riders with windswept hair gliding along with wide, toothy grins. Also gone was any hope that I would be able to use my phone, go on a quick beer run, or order pizza delivery. Instead there was a bumpy road with exotic plant life and unique-looking birds that had long, slender necks and shimmering feathers soaring skyward, unencumbered by the cityscapes that impede their acrobatic antics. Every once in a while, a sign would crop up with ominous names of destinations within the park, such as Hells Bay and Snake Bight. *I'm not sure I want to go that way*, I thought, chuckling at my predicament and starting to question my judgment in agreeing to come here. "Too late, I'm already in, and there's no turning back," I whispered with resignation. *Besides*, I thought, *people from all over the world would love to be in my seat—I'm in the Everglades!* Yahoooooo!

The road seemed like it went on forever, and with each passing mile, it became abundantly clear that there would be nothing remotely connected to the outside world in here. I started feeling apprehensive but decided to wait to pass judgment until we arrived at our destination. *Maybe all the people will be there, and something will emerge, like Emerald City,* I thought, trying to amuse myself and deflect the ever-increasing feeling of isolation. After nearly forty miles, I finally got my first peek at the entrance to Flamingo. There was a marina to our left and a vacant visitors' center to the right that appeared more like a Wild West ghost town, minus the tumbleweed, than a fabulous fishing destination. There were *some* signs of life, if you counted the black vultures that circled overhead and the occasional sound of flats boats chugging up Buttonwood Canal.

There was a ranger station that seemed open, and we meandered over. We found two officers in the building. "How can we help you?" the ranger asked.

"We'd like to camp here for a few days. How much would that be?"

"Well, it's off season, so it'll be half price," he replied. He handed Chris the rate list. After filling out instructions and various forms, we were required to drop our money into a silver tube located by the small house that we would pass just before the campground. My apprehension intensified as we turned into the campsite: we were greeted by a desolate area where everything was overgrown yet mysteriously welcoming. I put my brave face on and tried to be happy, even though there were only two other campers in an area with over two hundred campsites.

Anxiety covered my mind like cutthroat grass, while Chris continued to assure me we would be all right. *We are in the Everglades, and nobody knows we're here except for a pair of park rangers who have probably left for home by now,* I thought. I had woefully embarked on a trip that I wasn't prepared for. What did I expect, the Holiday Inn? "Hey, there's still a lot of daylight. Let's take the boat out!" Chris yelled from the camper door.

"OK, let's go," I replied, trying to get my mind off other things.

"We'll head across Florida Bay and maybe do some fishing near Cape Sable," Chris said, and off we went.

Our ride across Florida Bay was choppy, as a distant storm crept ever so close in our direction. "Do you want to turn around?" Chris yelled over the roar of the engine.

"No! Let's keep going!" I insisted. The storm drifted away, allowing us to admire a flock of roseate spoonbill flying across the sky, looking more like tufts of cotton candy than endangered birds as they slowly dissolved into the late-afternoon sky. It was in that moment that I settled in and marveled at how fortunate I was to live in an area where the imagery far exceeds that of any cinema offering I could think of.

Returning to our campsite, I tried really hard to hold on to that vision of beauty I had just admired as I trudged through the knee-high grasses, hoping that there was no hidden creature in my path. We were ceremoniously escorted into our camper by the friendly mosquitoes that gleefully entered without invitation. That evening we dined by the light of our citronella candle, munching on turkey sandwiches and drinking glasses of beer. I have discovered that Flamingo is probably one of the few places that you have to burn a citronella candle *inside* your camper.

As dusk's dark blanket began to cover the night sky, I peered from my window and curiously looked around for any sign of anything. Earlier in the day, it had been a scene of singing birds and rustling leaves and the sounds of roaring engines racing across Florida Bay, but now it had all grown eerily quiet. Warm yellows and lush greens were replaced with a deep-blue sky that served as a backdrop for the earthly objects that seemed to be embracing the end of their day.

As the last bit of light began to disappear, the jagged silhouettes of a thousand trees appeared like goblins in the night. *Why did I agree to this?* I thought. *This is* crazy. I understood that this was the Everglades. What did I expect? I didn't really know, exactly, but now I do. I would like to suggest another sign at the entrance that reads something like this: "Enter at your own risk. This is the wilderness, so forget about your tweets, FaceTime, or whatever else it is you do in the civilized world, and start looking at something very real. This place gives new meaning to the term *creature comforts*. Bravery is mandatory upon entering."

Naturally, worst-case scenarios ponded in my thoughts as Chris snored away in the other room. I started to imagine a skunk ape groaning outside my window as I ran for my flimsy camping frying pan, hoping to scare it off. And then there's the other nagging thought of a convict who recently escaped the confines of the local correctional facility, demanding food, refuge, and probably some mosquito repellent. The scenarios went on and on until finally the morning greeted me with a sense of rescue.

We spent the morning eating breakfast and talking about our plans for the day. I packed peanut-butter sandwiches and gathered our extra scarves and pants. "Don't forget the EPIRB," Chris said, as he continued his tasks. An EPIRB is a GPS-enabled rescue beacon. When the right button is pressed, the coast guard will find you and assist you, should you find yourself in a life-threatening situation. This device was serving a dual purpose on this trip, since we had no weapons (except for my frying pan and a couple of fillet knives). We could press the button should any nefarious individuals want to do us harm, or should we encounter peril while fishing.

Opening our camper proved to be a challenging affair. Immediately upon opening, I was attacked by those bloodthirsty mosquitoes. I jumped out, slammed the door, and braved the twenty-five yards across knee-high grass, leaping from one spot to the next so that I would not step on a slithering snake or an Everglades rodent. I felt like a running back bounding toward the goal as I arched myself over the gunnels of the boat. With one quick leap and a slip over the side, I made it. I envisioned an imaginary referee extending his arms skyward: touchdown! Once in the boat, I secured our EPIRB. I had to make a repeat performance back to the camper, except in reverse, sort of like a playback. It seems that the local mosquitoes drink DEET like an early-morning mimosa, intoxicating themselves while still attached to victims' arms.

We launched the boat in Buttonwood Canal, where a large crocodile appeared like a surfacing submarine and began to slowly propel itself in our direction. "OK, Chris, let's idle on now," I said, watching the ancient creature veer off toward the bank.

"Here, honey, you can drive," Chris said, letting go of the steering wheel.

"OK, move over," I said gleefully. "Look how pretty!" As I got deeper into the canal, I noticed I was having trouble differentiating land from water. It was as if we were floating over a Monet painting or sliding along on some kind of watery mirage. The canal seemed benumbed by its own banks, and there was not a hint of the sky's reflection, just a smeary blend of distorted tree limbs and crooked tree trunks. *Which way is up? Where is the water?* My mind started playing tricks on me, and I slowed down. "Just a second. I have to adjust my eyes." I said, squinting. Finally the trees thinned out, causing a burst of blue to appear.

"You can go fast now," Chris said, and the vistas along the bay came into view, disturbed only by the muted figures of fishermen beginning the tedious task of staking their claim on various spots along the way.

We headed toward Shark River, where there would be plenty of good areas and, according to a guy at the ramp, tarpon. We fished for snapper along the way and managed to hook some keepers that we placed in the live well. "OK, time to get to the river," Chris said, and he upped the shallow anchor. As we entered the river's mouth, we noticed a large area of turbulence in the water a few hundred yards from our location. We approached the cacophony slowly, as not to disturb whatever was causing it. As we got closer, Chris turned to me. In an excitedly hushed tone, he said, "It's tarpon, and lots of them!"

Chris positioned the boat several yards from the rolling tarpon. The river's surface churned with ripples and fins as we eased our way closer. Our presence went unnoticed by these leviathans of the deep, and Chris grew giddier by the minute. "Hey, why don't you use a Yo-Zuri?" he said, producing a strange, dark-silver plastic thing with dangling, lethal-looking treble hooks. The top of the lure clearly read *Yo-Zuri* in bold gold letters.

"Thank goodness fish can't read," I quipped. I reached for the plastic object. I wasn't sold on the idea at all.

"OK, honey, cast out in the middle and reel in. But be careful—that lure is expensive." *Oh sheesh*, I thought. *Now I have to worry about that?* I threw out the large object, unsure as to how any fish could see the thing as it sank into the dark, murky waters of Shark River. In a matter of seconds, I got the tug of a lifetime.

"Chris!" I screamed. I envisioned myself being tugged into the chilly waters face first. I had something! Meanwhile my line started to scream. *Wheeeeeeeezzz!* "What do I do?" I shouted, panicked. The spool rotated faster and faster.

"Play it, honey!" Chris screamed back, and with all my might, I flung the rod up and set the hook. *Boom!* From the water a mighty fish leaped out into the afternoon sky, appearing fearless as it arched and flipped its head from side to side. Everything went in slow motion from that moment. I held tight as the massive fish with expressionless eyes shifted in the air with as much bravado as an ancient gladiator. Fighting for its life, it twisted and turned and then fell hard, back into the water. I pulled my rod up, and suddenly the line went limp.

"You had him, honey!" Chris said. He hugged my moistened shoulders. I paused for a minute, recalling all those idle hours fantasizing about what I would do if I ever caught a tarpon, and I was disappointed in my handling of the fish. "Try it again!" Chris encouraged, noticing my defeated posture.

"That was life changing!" I said breathlessly. I reeled in the lure, which was miraculously still on my line, set my sights over the port side of the boat, and with a slow, surreal arch, my line was airborne again, zipping through the milky-gray sky and landing into the water. "One, two, three," I began to count, giving the lure a chance to entice. Before I could get to seven, my line buzzed and took off. In an instant another large tarpon catapulted out of the water, shaking fiercely. The contrast of its shiny silver body against a now darkened, stormy sky was unforgettable. My hook set perfectly as it fell back in, only to reappear in seconds like a missile. The fish flung itself as it flashed its anime eyes toward me, and then it fell once again, into the depths of Shark River.

By now a storm had started to creep up on us. My line held on to the tarpon that was now swimming toward our boat. "Here he comes," Chris yelled. "I'll pull the trolling motor!"

"Hurry!" I yelled. My rod had bent into a perfect arch. It looked like a tiny twig about to snap. I felt as though I had the upper hand as I held my ground and the fish paused. *Aha! I will have this fish up to the surface soon.* I grew with excitement at the thought of staring right into those saucer-sized eyes. My flimsy fifteen-pound test monofilament held on, proving its worth. Suddenly, out of the corner of my eye, I noticed a bright flashing followed by a thunderous applause, as if the approaching tempest was cheering on my efforts. A large white wall of rain was now quickly approaching: it appeared I was going to finish this fight in a torrential downpour. Chilly water began pelting my face. My biceps were bursting. "He's turning your way!" I yelled toward Chris, and he yanked up the trolling motor. Just as the last of the prop was clearing the water's edge, my line went limp. I fell backward as the heavy rain stuck me like tiny daggers.

"You had him up to the gunnels, honey," Chris yelled over the thunder, "and that counts." He continued calmly but sternly, "We better get out of here fast." And we left the storm in our foamy wake.

"Where are we going?" I yelled, trying to let go of my loss.

"To Graveyard Creek," Chris replied, his attention focused on navigating the boat.

"Graveyard Creek?" I yelled back with trepidation.

"Graveyard Creek is a place where there was a *real* murder," Chris said with a smile. He slowed the boat. "That's what I've been told."

"Yeah, *right*. Sounds like some fish tale to me. You know how fishermen like to embellish," I said with a smile, and we slipped through the creek's entrance, escaping the brunt of the storm.

With the heavy rains behind us, we trolled the area, keeping our eyes out for bait. Our shrimp supply was running low, and I was growing more skeptical about the possibility of catching anything. "Look! I think there's bait over there!" Chris said. He peered out over the horizon at a quivering on the water's surface. He quickly hoisted the trolling motor up, and we crept close to our target. With the precision of an Olympic disc thrower, Chris tossed the net high into the air, his brawny arms glistening. It made a whoosh before falling into the amber waters of Shark River.

"Do you think we got them?" I asked, breathless with anticipation.

"Well, let's see," Chris replied. There was a hint of confidence in his voice. As the net appeared on the surface, a large ball of slivering silver wiggled and flipped in its clutches. The weights that clasp together held the fishy treasure tightly. "Whoa, we are set for bait!" Chris said gleefully. He dumped the lively fish onto the deck and quickly scooped them up and placed them in the live well.

We now had serious bait. Visions of snook and redfish leaped around in my head, and I became intoxicated at the thought. "Let's troll these banks," Chris said from the bow. "I think you should put a split shot on your line instead of the half-ounce sinker you're using." He positioned the boat and headed parallel to the shoreline.

"Split shot? What the heck is a split shot?" I asked with some consternation. Change isn't easy for me when it comes to my fishing techniques, but so far Chris's suggestions have produced some pretty nice fish. "OK, I'll try. Can you put it on for me?" I asked coyly.

"Honey!" Chris groaned. "You know how to do that. Just look in the tackle box and look for the tiny weights." By this time of the day, I was growing tired and also a little troublesome.

"OK, I'll look," I replied, reaching into the box. "OK, how do you do this?" I said, lifting my line toward him. I held the tiny weight that was the size of a pearl between my forefinger and thumb.

He grabbed the line and the weight. "This is how," he said. He placed the groove of the gray metal ball against the thin line and squeezed it together. "There," he said, casting his eyes toward the greenish-brown landscape. "Now you're good to go."

Looking at my split shot, I wondered how in the world the thing would sink at a reasonable depth. Chris guided the trolling motor near the banks of a densely packed mangrove island, where the red roots arched out like the legs of a hairy tarantula. "Now how does this work?" I asked. There was a tinge of annoyance in my voice even though I was trying to be sensible.

"OK, just cast toward the bank, and reel in slowly," Chris said with a renewed enthusiasm. I'm not one who likes to troll, but to display some solidarity with Chris, I nodded my head with a reassuring shake and started the process of casting into the green abyss, hoping that I wouldn't hook a tree limb.

Casting can be as difficult or as easy as you make it. You can toss the line out gently and not expect anything, or you can fiercely throw it with the strength of ten men and expect everything. I adopted the gentle toss, trying to conserve what little energy I had left. We were still far from the ramp, and I had grown chilly. I felt as stiff as a half-frozen fillet when my line came to an abrupt halt. "Oh damn! I'm stuck on a root," I groaned. I gently tugged the line, trying to coax it out of its captor's grasp, when it started to wiggle. Seconds later the battle was on.

It wasn't a root, but a red—a very large redfish. "Chris, hurry! Help! I have a—." I couldn't get any words to come out due to my struggle to hold on as the fish jigged and jagged with as much force as an out-of-control freight train.

"Hold it, honey! Don't horse it around," Chris yelled. He headed toward the stern to try to net the fish.

"I'm not horsing it," I yelled, gulping for oxygen. There's a strategy to landing a fish, and I'm still working on my fisherman's finesse.

"He's under the boat!" Chris's voice was urgent. "You're going to lose it if you don't get him out from under—." Chris dropped to his stomach with net in hand and dipped the net far under the stern, scooping up the powerful red. "I got it!" he yelled, and he lifted the heavy fish onto the deck. "Wow, honey, nice fish!" The ruby-red catch flopped against the white deck, trying its best to escape.

The ride back to the ramp was chilly, and I was relieved when I spotted Buttonwood Canal. "Thank goodness we made it," I groaned. I stretched my legs and let out a big yawn. The boat idled along, and we scurried about, trying to gather our shoes, wallets, phones, and any other items that needed to be secured or put away. As we approached the dock, a man with a floppy hat waved his arms toward us and yelled something. "What's he saying?" I asked Chris. My furrowed brow crinkled at the thought of possible problems. I wasn't in any mood to have any issues. I was tired, hungry, soaked, sunburned, and done.

"The birds are eating your truck!" yelled the middle-aged man. "That's your truck, right?" he continued, gesturing toward our silver Silverado, which was parked all alone in a secluded area.

"What the heck is that?" I whispered to myself. I jumped onto the deck while Chris secured the boat. I picked up the pace as the scene unfolded before me. Yes, there were vultures *eating* our truck! I was bewildered at the sight of black feathers with pecking beaks that sounded like jackhammers pounding on a tin roof. *Ting! Ting! Ting! Ting!*

"Shoo!" I yelled angrily toward the birds. "Scram!" I yelled louder, frantically waving my arms. To my surprise, their crinkly gray heads just kept pounding. They hardly noticed my disdain for their behavior until I got close and swatted a few times.

One by one, the feathery fiends hopped off nonchalantly and half flew, half walked to the nearest tree and stared in my direction. Stunned at what had just happened, I glanced over toward the dock. I heard the man with the floppy hat talking to Chris.

"I guess you missed that sign over there," he said, pointing toward a faded white building. The sign indicated that the birds can destroy your vehicle and it was advisable to use the provided blue tarps. There, in the weathered brown bin, was a mound of tarps that were used to protect vehicles from truck-eating birds. The odd thing about this whole fiasco was that I *had* noticed the sign, but I'd thought it was a joke. I wasn't laughing now. I wasn't sure how we would make an insurance claim, considering I would have to explain to the agent that a flock of birds ate my truck.

Chris approached with trepidation, but he decided that the damage wasn't too severe. As it turned out, the birds had somehow developed a taste for the rubber lining. I'm not sure why, considering the plethora of food sources in the area. "OK, let's get back to camp," Chris said, and he tossed the rods in the back and hopped in.

Our campsite sat in the brilliance of the fading afternoon light, and the majestic gumbo-limbo tree that was positioned near us glistened as the last rays of the day covered its smooth, reddish trunk. "I love that tree," I exclaimed. "It's just so magical!"

Chris nodded in agreement as he entered the camper and began to unload the items from his pockets. "Let's go to town and get some supplies," he said. "We need milk and a few other things."

"OK," I said, not thinking too much about it.

Our trip to Florida City went rather quickly, considering it's about ninety miles round trip, give or take a few. We talked about our fishing adventure as we drove and couldn't stop laughing as we recounted certain aspects of the day that provided some unforgettable moments. Suddenly, as we made our turn into Everglades National Park, a feeling of unease swept over me.

"Honey, I can't see anything except for what's in front of our headlights," I said with a slight hint of fear. Our laughter turned to an uncomfortable silence, and I tried my best to make small talk even though I had a big problem with the situation. I no longer had phone service, and the easygoing feel of swaying grasses and flying birds was gone, replaced by nothing but a few fading stars and the ghostly gray ahead. Darkness was upon us.

As we approached the entrance to Flamingo, the dimly lit street glowed an ominous color, and the large trees created scary shadows along the road. "There's nobody here," I said, my voice rising with concern. "Chris, I don't know if I can do this." My eyes widened with worry. We were the only campers left in the park.

"Do what, honey? There's nothing to worry about. Relax!" he replied. He made the turn into our campsite. As we pulled in, the darkness was disturbed by another pair of headlights. They slowly circled our camper and then abruptly parked right in front of it.

"Chris, who is that? What are they doing? They aren't campers!" I nearly came off my seat with terror. There was nobody to hear us should there be any trouble, and we had nothing to defend ourselves with.

"Honey, stop it!" Chris yelled. "You are overreacting. Although I do have to admit, this is a little strange." His voice had a hint of anxiety. "Well, I have to get our fillet knives."

"OK," I said, shaking, "but hurry up." As Chris pulled up, I dove to the floorboard. I was not about to let this mysterious person know that I was a girl. For all he knew, I was a strapping six-foot-four young man, not a five-feet-five wisp of a woman with dull fingernails and an arthritic hip.

To add to my frustration, the interior light stayed on for a few seconds, illuminating my cover before finally fading out. Darn those interior lights! If this stranger wanted to do me harm, now was the time for him to take a chance. A tidal wave of adrenaline surged through my body. The fight-or-flight instinct took over as I peered over the dashboard. I could tell it was a man with thinning hair, and he was looking in his van's rearview mirror toward our camper. "OK," I whispered to myself, "if he gets out, I'll be ready to throw some punches, kick him in the groin, and cuss."

After what seemed like an eternity, Chris jumped back into the truck with knives in hand. "I'm not staying here!" I yelled with a kind of assertiveness that I rarely use when I'm talking to Chris. "I feel like I'm in some scary movie plot and I'm the next victim! I want to leave *now*!"

"We have to fillet the fish first," Chris said. There was little emotion in his voice.

"OK, but after that we *leave*!" I replied flatly.

We approached the fillet house that sits next to Buttonwood Canal, and I peered through the torn screen. The broken door creaked as the soft evening wind gently pushed it open. "Let's do this," Chris said. We fumbled around and found a light switch and began the task of filleting the fish. "Damn, I wish I would have sharpened these," Chris said. His aggravation seemed to grow. I'm not sure what he was more annoyed with—his dull knives or my fearful neurosis. He continued his best with our fish as I kept watch for the mysterious man in the white van. From the darkness of the mouth of the campsite, headlights slowly emerged.

"Chris, we're in trouble. He's heading our way!" I yelled.

I started to look for potential escape routes. As far as I could see, we had two choices: we could jump into the crocodile-infested canal or take on the creepy guy. It looked like we were going to have to take on the creepy guy. I reasoned that if I had to go down, I might as well go down swinging and not be eaten. I started to laugh to myself—not a funny laugh, but a laugh that comes from a scary place.

"Hey look—he's going the other way!" Chris said with some relief. At that point nothing was making any sense. I was delirious with fear and wanted to cry as I continued to roll up my sleeves.

We were once again alone. My adrenaline had calmed down just enough that I was starting to feel the nagging, itching welts from the mosquito brigade that had staked its claim on my exposed flesh.

"OK, let's go," Chris said, and I jumped into the driver's seat. Chris had not realized how serious I was until I floored it and took off like a rocket. "Slow down!" he interjected.

"I'm leaving! I am *not* going back there! I want to *go* home or somewhere other than here!" I yelled in one long diatribe filled with gasps of air. Chris and I argued as I sped down the bumpy road out of Everglades National Park with boat in tow. "I'll find a hotel," I said angrily.

"No, I don't want to pay for a hotel. We have *a campsite*!" Chris said. There was some conviction in his voice, enough to push me more over the edge. I already was jacked up and was in no mood to negotiate. "Hey look! There's a car," Chris said. "I bet that's him!"

"OK, we are going to pass," I said, pressing the gas down, "and don't *look* at him!"

I really had no time to think about my rate of speed or anything else, and I was grateful that his vehicle had slowed to a crawl. By now Chris had calmed me down. He has a way with me that I can't explain, but it was working. We decided to hole up in a secluded area, turn our lights out, and wait for him to pass. As his vehicle drove by, Chris said, "See? I told you he was leaving the park. He's probably some fisherman dragging his feet to go home. Let's go back to camp. You are overreacting!" I waited until I was absolutely sure he was gone, flicked my lights on, took a deep breath, and headed back to Flamingo.

"I'm glad you feel better," Chris lovingly said as we rounded the corner that led to our camper. I began to find calmness in my thoughts and knew that my husband would never put me in harm's way.

"OK, honey," I sighed. "I'll try my best to be a little more reasonable," I said softly, and I turned into the darkness.

"Look at that!" Chris yelled. "There's a huge owl standing at our door!" To my surprise a very large owl stood silently and held its ground even though our headlights illuminated the massive bird. Its large eyes never blinked as it lifted its expansive wings and took to the tree that was leaning toward our camper.

"Hey, that's my angel!" I quipped happily.

"Oh, OK, honey. I'm beat. Let's go to bed," Chris said. He opened the camper, tugged at his shirt, and headed for the bed. I swear he started to snore even before hitting his pillow! I grabbed the pull-out couch and flopped down, trying to blot out what had just happened. *I am staying here, and that's the end of it*, I said to myself. *I am going fishing tomorrow with my husband, and I will catch something big, I will catch something big*, I repeated to myself sleepily, and all went dark.

The next thing I knew, I was awakening to the warming light of another day. I twisted around and realized I had fallen asleep fully clothed and with my shoes still on. I lifted my head up and peered out the window, where I saw the old gumbo-limbo standing strong, serenely swaying in the morning breeze. I was still shaken from the night before, but I wanted to try to be strong for Chris. After a much-needed shot of caffeine and some hot breakfast, we got the boat in the water and took off for Harney River, one of Chris's favorite spots.

"We'll take the back way to get to Harney," Chris said. He adjusted his seat and said with certainty, "We got a good day, and we should be able to catch some nice fish."

"Great," I said, and he pushed the throttle forward. It's hard to talk over the roar of the engine, and for the most part I sat in silence, taking in all the beauty of the backcountry and making nautical notes for future reference. After a lengthy ride, we turned toward the mouth of the river and idled in. There was nothing unusual about this setting except for a large white object that rested against a cluster of mangroves about one hundred yards from us. Harney River is considered a remote location, so naturally I was apprehensive when Chris decided to get a closer look.

"Chris, forget about that, *please?*" My request fell on deaf ears. He inched the boat nearer to what appeared to be an abandoned cabin cruiser.

"Look at that—it's a boat. I wonder if anybody's in there," he said, grinning mischievously. "I'll honk the horn and see if anyone comes out."

"No! Stop! Don't do that!" I yelled angrily. "There might be somebody with a gun. Or—worse—there could be dead bodies in that cabin!"

"Oh, coooool. Dead bodies!" he said, making creepy hand motions and laughing.

"Stop it!" I yelled back at him, swatting in his direction.

"Oh, c'mon, honey. Let's go aboard and check it out." Chris was wearing a Cheshire-cat grin. This boat *radiated* trouble from its bow to its stern, and I was not about to let Chris get any closer to it. "Oh, OK, honey, but I'm going to honk the horn!" He sounded two long beeps, laughing.

"Chris, *stop* it! Stop!" He continued to laugh as he trolled away, into the horizon of just another day in this unpredictable world.

We didn't catch the fish we'd thought we would, but our day was eventful nonetheless. We discovered an abandoned boat, saw a crocodile, and observed playful dolphin. Chris gave me the wheel for a while, and I zipped along, trying to remember our path so that I could use my brain as a GPS instead of the computer on board. Approaching the dock, I reminded Chris about our plan to fish, pack up the camper, and leave. He could see that I had grown exhausted from a day in the heat and was tired from the exertion of casting, throwing an anchor, and being bounced around on choppy waters. Using his usual charm, he convinced me that it was probably best to stay another night. As I stepped off the boat and started walking like an emperor penguin back to the truck, I had to agree. I was stiff. I was ready to eat and go to bed. If there were any crazy beings out this evening, so be it. At that point I didn't give a rip.

The next day, while wrapping up all the hoses and packing away the last of the items from the camper, I took one long look around at the overgrown grasses and the trees that gracefully swished and swirled with every gust of the fall breeze. Before leaving, Chris wanted to stop at the ranger's office. While looking at some handouts, he took the opportunity to discuss with the officer what had happened the night before with the strange man.

"It's probably somebody looking for snakes," he assured us. "Nothing ever happens here except for fishing."

"See, honey? I *told* you there was nothing to worry about," Chris said, smiling as he gently patted my shoulder.

"OK," I said. "No big deal."

Reflecting on the last few days at Flamingo, I would say that it was a lot like my first ride on Disney World's Space Mountain. As a teenage girl, I had no idea what to expect, but I was not about to chicken out when the time came to get on board. Strapped into the small seat, my best friend, Pam, and I readied ourselves for the unknown. After the ride we screamed in unison, "Let's do that again!" We had discovered that it was everything we had hoped for: fast, loud, and frightfully exhilarating, with unforgettable twists and turns.

By the time it was time to leave, I had come to realize that Flamingo was not only a trip about fishing. It was a trip about overcoming fear while experiencing the unpredictable path of roads less traveled, including the twists and turns. *Will I ever come back here?* I wondered as I glanced toward the flurry of fishermen readying their boats with rods, buckets, sunblock, and lunches. My mind went blank momentarily and then reemerged with a nostalgic nod. *Yes, I will do that again…but probably during peak camping season,* I laughed to myself as I buckled up for the ride home.

CHAPTER 8

─── ✤ ───

The Smell of Rum

LIKE A CAGED animal, I paced back and forth in our camper, waiting for that one moment when my escape would be certain. *I have to get out there and start fishing*, I thought as my impatience grew. The first rays of morning had peeked over the mangrove islands, and I felt like the day was already half over. Chris had left nearly forty minutes earlier and should have been home already.

As I busied myself with packing lunches, the camper door began to creak open. It was Chris, and I could tell right away that something was amiss by the way his head was turned downward. "What's the matter?" I asked.

"There's no bait, so we're going to have to wait a little while," he said apologetically.

I was growing more annoyed with the passing of each boat that hurried across Chokoloskee Bay and disappeared into the hazy horizon. I could see everything from my vantage point, including the men in their flats boats who were tying knots and checking their coolers. I decided to try to distract myself by helping to clean up the camper and assisting Chris with various boating details. Mike DeVestern, a friend of Chris's, had joined us for this trip, and I welcomed the extra help. Throwing the anchor and pulling it back in sure can grow tiresome.

Our delay was thankfully short. The bait truck arrived not long after Chris had returned, and we bought about two hundred shrimp. We finished packing the cooler and placed our rods neatly in their slots, where they stood like soldiers at the ready. Preparation goes a long way when it comes to fishing. The last thing you want to do when you arrive at the first fishing hole is mess with your tackle box, rummaging around for hooks and sinkers like it's some bargain-basement clutter box. What a waste of fishing time!

The trip had begun in earnest, and waves from the Gulf of Mexico doused our deck with their salty liquid. To pass the time, I made an attempt to examine my lines to check for any imperfections. Just then a gust of wind blew forcefully across the deck, rattling my pole and causing me to take a tumble. "Whoops!" I yelled toward Chris, who was paying little attention to my antics. He and Mike were busy manning the helm and carrying on like merry marauders as they checked the chartsand discussed what kind of fish might be hitting the hook once we anchored up in Lostmans River.

After navigating successfully through the shallows and the shoals, we anchored up at one of Chris's favorite spots. In a matter of minutes, everything started biting. Permit, mangrove snapper, sheepshead, trout, horseflies, and the wind. Thank goodness for the blustery breeze; without that we all would have been carried off by the mutant mosquitoes. I retreated momentarily to layer my clothing. I fished out my red bell-bottom sweatpants and a sweatshirt and promptly put them on. They were a bit heavy for this time of year, but I had come to the conclusion that I would rather sweat than scratch. I found it slightly amusing to hear the guys cuss under their breath as they smacked at their flesh, trying their best to ward off attacks from the pesky horseflies. They had forgone the extra clothes. In their defense, the air temperature was about ninety degrees—that could've been the reason they didn't opt for extra clothing. Once layered, I turned my full attention to my fishing technique and had little time to spend worrying about them or the sweat that was now pouring profusely down my furrowed brow.

I'll cast over there, I thought as I eyed the jagged branches that were partly submerged. *I bet there's a snapper over there.*

Just as I was about to zing my line toward my designated target, Chris quietly crooned, "Honey, there are a lot of snags over there. Why don't you put on a popping cork?"

"I don't have time to do that," I replied flatly, and I let my line fly. My mind had entered the fishing zone, and I didn't want to be bothered. After I casually rebuffed his advice, he turned his attention back to Mike. They began to banter. One minute they were talking serious fish talk, and the next minute they would quarrel like a pair of old biddies, all the while confidently casting toward the textured tawny banks. I marveled at their multitasking skills as they vied for voice volume.

"Okaaaay," I interjected when I'd had enough. It was tough trying to concentrate when two grown men were discussing fishing nuances in a lively manner. Eventually the two went their separate ways, each claiming a new spot to fish.

"I want a reel screamer!" Mike yelled, and he cast his jig into the open water.

Chris heaved his line toward the shoreline and began pulling in keeper-sized snapper faster than a county fair auctioneer can talk. "I knew this spot would be good!" he ballyhooed.

The snapper and sheepshead were hitting hard off the banks of Lostmans River, but Mike continued throwing his lure out into the middle. "I got one!" he hollered, his pole bent downward.

"I'll get the net," Chris yelled back. Mike was taking his time, nonchalantly revolving his caster with a large fish in tow. "You better hurry and get that fish up to the gunnel," Chris said.

"Yeah, I got it," Mike replied, confident. He began to reel faster, and the line suddenly snapped, freeing its unwitting passenger. He groaned loudly at his folly while Chris stood motionless, holding the net that was to scoop up the hefty catch. I said nothing as I sat on the gunnel, hoping to distance myself from this dispiriting outcome.

I turned my energies back to the banks and began to concentrate on feeling the bite of a fish. My obedient monofilament looked taut and ready to give me a signal. An ever-so-tiny twitch stirred the water, and my line gave me the nod. I yanked my rod sideways and came up empty.

"You have to set the hook," Mike chimed happily in my direction. I was slightly startled at the notion that my blunder had been observed but politely nodded in his direction and acknowledged his suggestion.

"She catches plenty of fish," Chris said, casting his eyes toward Mike. "She doesn't need any instructions." I just rolled my eyes and smiled at the pair. After all this time, I'm still confused about the techniques that guys talk about concerning setting a hook. I just tug when I feel a tug, sort of like a game of tug-of-war. Sometimes I win, and sometimes the fish do. You can call it what you want.

The watery rush hour in Lostmans River was coming to an end, and the quick-running outgoing tide headed to the Gulf, seemingly taking the fish with it. We were now facing the quandary of dealing with the falling tide. Chris began deftly maneuvering our Pathfinder 24, hugging the banks and gingerly finding the path toward the wilderness waterway. He successfully navigated us to the fuller bays, and our pace slowed slightly to take in the serendipitous scene.

"We'll head over there and fish some," Chris said. He pointed the boat in the direction of a tranquil-looking creek. We approached the entrance quietly, allowing the slow tide to carry us to our spot. Chris downed the shallow anchor, and we readied our poles to cast into the maple-colored waters. Along the bank there was activity, and we knew that there must be some predators swimming around. We solved that mystery quickly when Chris instantly hooked into a chunky mangrove snapper.

The bites began to slow, and we were making plans to leave when I noticed a strong wake coming toward us from the other side of the small creek. The sight of this anomalous water pattern struck me as peculiar, considering the tide was moving the opposite direction. *There must be something sizable coming toward us*, I thought. Seconds after my observation, a ghostly white dolphin appeared from the shallows, barely able to stay submerged, and flashed by our boat like a bolt of lightning. The boat rocked from the force of its wake.

"Whoa! A white dolphin!" I shrieked.

"Yeah, how about that?" Chris replied. We paused for a moment, trying to comprehend what had just happened. The boat continued to rock gently from the aquatic apparition's haste. "Let's get out of here before another one decides to come passing through," Chris said jokingly, and we lifted the anchor and left.

We began the last part of our trek heading north through the waters that serve as a tollgate for the myriad of fish that feed and breed there. As we made our way through the shoal waters, I noticed juvenile snapper, snook, and a school of young mullet gliding with the soft current and quickly heading for the safety of the mangrove roots that reach out for them like a mother's arm. Our voyage continued through a crooked creek, where the abundance of trees took on a life of their own. With each bend of the creek, I took a look at a different tree. One looked like an aging man sporting a long, graying beard, another resembled a ballerina frozen in a perfect arabesque, and the one next to that appeared snakelike. As we forged through, I relished the brief jaunt through the leafy labyrinth, appreciating the shade it provided and the quiet reflection.

"OK, honey, it's almost time to get the poles ready, the end of the creek is just ahead," Chris said, jarring me from my reverie.

It had been a little over ten hours since we'd set out to prove our fishing prowess, and I had grown weary. Time means nothing to you out there; only the tides command attention. *Where does the time go?* I'm continually amazed at the passing of moments when I'm working the banks, but once you put your rod in its holder for the last time, *that's* when the pains of your exertion reveal themselves. Those tiny cuts in your hands really start to burn at day's end, when your attention has a chance to wander. Seated, allowing the wind to blow through my salt-scented hair and cool my sweat-covered face, I vowed to pace myself in a more intelligent manner in our next outing.

"We did really good these last couple of days," I said to Chris. He was in the middle of navigating us toward Chokoloskee Bay.

"Yeah, between all of us we have some pretty nice fish," he boastfully responded. After we docked, I hosed off our reels, ridding them of their salty covering, while Chris busied himself flushing out the engine. Mike retrieved the fillet knives to help out with the filleting duties. By day's end, as the last of the rods were put away, our camper began to fill with laughter, the smell of fish frying, and the exotic scent of rum as the sun's final rays began to extinguish into the western waters of Chokoloskee Bay.

CHAPTER 9

Barracuda

WITH A LIVE well full of shrimp and a bag of chum, Chris and I set off into the high tide of Coon Key, making our way to West Pass River. We hadn't planned to fish deep in the belly of the Gulf of Mexico, but we were enticed by the glass-like surface of the water. "Let's head out to the tower. You know—those air force towers I told you about," Chris yelled excitedly. "It's smooth enough out here. What say you?" His pleading eyes left me no other option but to say yes.

Our destination was about thirty miles offshore, and this new experience challenged my fortitude. "Start looking for the tower. We should see it soon," Chris yelled over the thumping rhythm of the boat against the rushing water. We motored quickly along into a monochromatic canvas, where sky and sea blended seamlessly. I had to blink occasionally to keep my perspective. Glancing toward the northwest, I saw something from my cooler seat that looked like an ancient obelisk standing tall, unbothered by the winds and waves of its surroundings.

"Chris, is this OK—to be here near this tower?" I asked cautiously.

"Of course," he replied, and he threw out the anchor. After securing the boat, we baited up and began our fishing in earnest. Then unexpected company arrived, flashing hungry eyes.

The menacing fish resembled Scud missiles as they headed straight for the bow and then, as if programed, split up and circled the boat. "Chris, look. What are they?" I whispered.

Giving one glance over the side, he passively replied, "Oh, that's barracuda."

"Barra...barra...cuda?" I stammered. Fear began washing over me like the spray of cool water that sprang from the bow with each rolling wave.

48

Maybe this wasn't a good idea, I thought as I looked out upon the horizon, realizing that land was nowhere in sight.

I sauntered back to the stern as if nothing was wrong. "OK, let's do some fishing," I exclaimed, boldly trying my best to ignore the sea monsters with flying-saucer eyes that continued hovering near. *Hovering? Why do they hover? They're loitering! Aren't they supposed to be swimming or something?* I thought.

"What's wrong, honey?" Chris asked, noticing my stoic stance.

"Nothing. Nope, nothing," I quickly replied. I went about the business of baiting my hook.

"Throw over there," Chris said, pointing to the base of the tower. "There might be some snapper." I glanced nonchalantly into the water and noticed that the barracuda had left.

"Thank goodness," I sighed, and then cast my line. Before the bait had a chance to get wet, my reel started to scream. "Chris!" I yelped, just as a large barracuda shot out from the sea and soared by our heads with anger in its eyes and my hook in its mouth. I could feel the water fly off its flesh as it went skyward and dove back down into the depths, trying to take me with it. "Chris, help!" I screamed. My rod appeared small against the backdrop of the Gulf of Mexico. I held tight, worrying about what to do. *Should I let go? No, that wouldn't do!* I did the next best thing I could come up with: I yelled for my husband. "Chris, take my rod! Hurry!"

"You got this! Run over here and *take* it!" he instructed encouragingly. Just as I was ready to thrust the rod into his abdomen, the line went limp. "You should have jumped up on the bow and fought it," Chris said, shaking his head, puzzled by my lack of fishing bravado.

Who said fishing wasn't an extreme sport? I thought, breathlessly trying to get Chris to help me sit down. I'd always thought I could fish with the big boys, undaunted. Yet there I was, trembling, cold, and beaten.

After a few minutes, the wind picked up, and so did my resolve. "I'm not letting a bunch of barracuda intimidate me," I mumbled. I stood up, brushed myself off, and went back at it, this time with amped-up swagger. I baited my hook once again and threw caution to the wind. *I'm ready this time*, I thought. I didn't hook any barracuda, but the blue runners were hitting hard. We caught quite a few and released them back into the water.

"Hey, do you want to learn how to use a sabiki?" Chris asked.

"What's a sabiki?" I replied with little interest. Bobbing with the waves from the Gulf of Mexico, I noticed there wasn't anything or anybody as far as the eye could see.

"Here, watch this," he said. He held up tiny lures that resembled opal earrings on a chain with a weight on the end of it. He dropped the string into the water, jiggled it, and pulled up several blue runners at once.

"That looks fun. Yeah, I'll try," I said, taking the sabiki to the other side.

While pulling up slowly, I thought I saw a dark shadow move under the boat. *Hmm, maybe it was the shadow of a cloud*, I thought. I felt a tug on the sabiki and started pulling it to the surface when a sinister shadow appeared below, like black ink oozing from a broken pen. Paralyzed by fear, I watched the darkness spread out long and wide, about half the size of our boat. And then I saw its round, colorless eye.

"Chris!" I yelled. "Chris!" Without warning, the large, slow-moving beast sank quickly, leaving a large wake. Our boat felt like an out-of-control carnival ride.

"What's the matter?" he said, rushing over after placing his rod down.

"There was this…thing—a *big* thing. I've never seen something like that in the water!"

"Oh, I bet it was a jewfish. They get pretty big," he said, brushing off the idea of anything more. "Now we know what was breaking our lines."

The waves started rolling bigger now, and we decided, for our safety, that it was time to go. That was fine with me. I'd had enough of flying barracuda and large beasts with colorless eyes. Chris turned our Pathfinder east, and, to my relief, we headed for land. Looking toward the cloudless sky, I had time on the long boat ride to reassess my fishing skills and lack thereof. I started a list of pros and cons in my head. I went for the cons list first, since it was easier to compile: there's the mosquitoes, the sweat stinging my eyes, strong currents, heavy winds, thunderstorms out in the open, dodging lightning bolts, rigging, rerigging, the top of the high tide, the bottom of the low tide, slack tide, cut fingers, skinny water, frozen bait, trying to pull anchor off a bottom of rocks, going home with no keeper-sized fish, getting tangled in Chris's line, catfish, casting into a tree, breaking a line just as I get my fish up to the gunnels, and summer sun's burning, searing rays. It's a wonder I even *go* fishing. I laughed out loud over the roar of the engine. Oddly, everything I had on my con list was also on the pro side. Fishing is nothing like I thought it would be. It's an endless adventure with many challenges that can't be defined by the line or what's on the end of it.

"OK, let's head to Fakahatchee and see what's over there," Chris said. He slowed the engine. "But first, can you pass me a sandwich?" It was lunchtime, and the tide was beginning to slow down. After fishing in the Gulf, this back-country girl happily looked toward the islands that were now in view. With a sandwich in one hand and my rod in the other, I started thinking about the fish I was going to catch while admiring the lush, green landscape that laid out before me like a welcome mat.

CHAPTER 10

Redfisher

A SENSE OF misgivings flooded my mind as we headed to Fort Myers Marine in Fort Myers, Florida, to pick up a new boat. Our decision to downsize to a Hewes Redfisher came after it occurred to us that our current boat was to big for our new lot in Chokoloskee and the drudgeries of cleaning, detailing, and organizing our Pathfinder 24 had grown too big for what little time we could give it. Fishing does not end when the lines are reeled in. The process can continue well into the next day, as you muscle off the last bit of catfish slime; haul out bunches of bags containing half-eaten sandwiches, banana peels, and crumpled chip bags; gather the tackle boxes and smelly fish rags; search for missing shoes, nets, and lures; sponge out the compartments; and flush out the engine.

Traveling along the road toward our destination, I shifted in my seat and took a moment to glance back at the yellow boat as it faithfully followed us. I grew more melancholy by the minute. I had fond memories of my grandchildren, Travis, Caleb, and Greyson, running barefoot along the deck, laughing as they lifted up their catch while my daughter Delia cheered them on. I smiled as I recalled wiping up spilled drinks along our deck while watching peanut-butter fingers try hard to bait their own hooks. I quietly bewailed the thought that there probably wouldn't be any more family adventures in the new boat. It was just too small to accommodate everybody. Chris had just started to teach his grandkids, Charlotte and Grayson (yes, the spelling is different from my grandson Greyson), something about fishing, and that was coming to end as well.

Upon our arrival at Fort Myers Marine, we were guided to Greg, our orientation designee, who began his tutorial with a wide grin, standing barefoot on the bow of the boat. "Oh, you're going to love this boat," he said with a mischievous chuckle. "You're going to just *love* her."

He talked about our boat in the feminine, something mariners have done for centuries. I couldn't help but find it mildly nostalgic. I envisioned hearty sailors at sea with the woman they loved—even if she had wooden planks and creaky parts. I became intoxicated with every sip of his words that he laughingly ladled out like grog on a ship.

"Be real easy with her at first," he said in a more hushed tone. "Take your time with her, and she'll do you right," he continued, tinkering with the wires under one of the compartments.

After a few minutes of adjustments, he sat upright and gazed out the garage door, where young men were milling about the larger boats on display. "You know," he said in a blissful tone, "this is my dream boat." His voice dropped to a murmur, and he stroked the side gunnel with admiration. "You're going to just love her." After a few more instructions, we wrapped up the tutorial and eased our way back onto the cold concrete floor.

Our first few outings with the Redfisher went well, and I was ready to embrace the new memories that it would provide. I had grown to appreciate the intimate experience of a smaller boat and its performance in shallow water. In the Hewes, our surroundings always seemed much larger as we drifted along the rivers: bigger sky, bigger islands—even the fish appeared bigger. Our Hewes was ready to accommodate one other passenger, and we welcomed my daughter Anna aboard during her brief vacation from the Midwest.

Our first day out, we launched into a crisp breeze and glided across the calm waters of Chokoloskee Bay, headed toward a tableau of mangrove islands that blended into the sky. We had our poles ready as Chris made his first stop at a fishing spot where we'd caught keeper snapper. "OK, Anna. Here you go," he said, handing her a shrimp. After a few casts that came up empty, we decided that the fish hadn't arrived there yet, pulled anchor, and left. We idled slowly for a few minutes and discussed our next plan. We decided that we would do some sightseeing and forego fishing for the time being.

"Hey, Anna," I yelled over the roar of the engine, "we're almost to Alligator Creek. It *actually* has alligators that live there!" Anna smiled back toward me and nodded hesitantly. We silently twisted through the tiny creek, keeping a watchful eye for any alligators that could be lurking nearby. The silence of the scene was disturbed only by the sloshing of the waters that swept against the banks.

"Let's drop anchor here," Chris said, his words blending in with the purring sound of the power pole sinking into the copper water.

Chris cast his line toward the bank as I continued the process of getting bait for Anna and myself. "I got something!" Chris yelled. As he reeled in, a large splash disturbed the surface, followed by a brief thrashing. And then it was over. "Whoa! An alligator tried to steal my fish! Look! There it is!" We quickly turned our heads and saw the reptile playing it cool in the shadows. Everything happened so fast, there was no time to react.

"Anna, get your camera! Here it comes!" I said. The crocodilian cavalry was heading our way. Like paparazzi attending a premiere, we clicked away toward the reptilian star from every conceivable angle. The gator would slowly swish to and fro, posing gracefully for us as we continued our photographic frenzy. But after a few moments of accommodating our clicks, the alligator lost interest, turned to the green curtain of the mangroves, and silently retreated into the shadows once again.

"Let's head to Gulf and try a few casts out there," Chris said.

"Good idea. Let's go!" I concurred.

Our Redfisher sped along in a westerly direction as we wound our way through the polychrome paths before us. The Gulf was softly rolling as we made our way to a park-boundary marker and anchored the boat. We baited up in unison and cast our hopes into the depths. Anna was trying her best, but I could tell her doubts were growing about hooking a fish. She had sat down, indicating to me that her enthusiasm was waning. I said nothing and kept watch on our surroundings. "Uh...um, I think I got something!" Anna said. She fumbled with her reel and regrouped quickly, pulling in a blue runner. After a few high fives, we released the fish and headed back to camp.

Our second day out on the water took us to some familiar territory near West Pass River. The river's not far from Chokoloskee and gave us an opportunity to hit some of the islands for bait. We idled toward Picnic Key, where we noticed quivering on the water's edge, indicating that bait was available. I tossed our heavy anchor out into the sand and then dropped the shallow anchor. The tide was coming in fast, so we had to work quickly. Chris made several attempts and changed his tactic after coming up empty.

"I'm heading over there," he mumbled, the salty net clenched between his teeth. "Follow me." I tiptoed silently and watched his body twist fervently as a blur of white rotated high into the afternoon sky and then silently fell into the sepia sea. He tugged hard at the net, pulled it toward the shore, and began to gloat. "Wow, we are *set* for bait!" he exclaimed. A mass of shiny fingerlings wiggled helplessly in the mesh of their captor's clutches.

We began our retreat from Picnic Key after releasing the anchor from the wet sand. "Hurry up, Anna. Get in the boat!" Chris yelled, and she scampered onto the bow. "Now that we have this good bait, we'll try one of our redfish spots." We sped off toward the east. Chris glanced at our depth finder as he approached our destination. "We can drop the shallow anchor here," he said, looking my way. "Let me know when it's all the way down."

I turned to watch it sink and noticed that it was already submerged. *Hmmm, that was really fast,* I thought.

"Chris, it's already down," I said, puzzled. I quietly gasped. *I forgot to pull up the shallow anchor!* I sat ruefully, angered by own gaffe, and wondered what I was going to say to Chris, who continued to push the down button.

"Well?" he asked, bemused at my hesitant response.

"Um, Chris, I think we have a problem," I said sheepishly. The dark metal pole protruded unnaturally and hung like a broken arm. "I think I forgot to bring the shallow anchor up when we left Picnic Key," I said, somewhat fessing up to my blunder.

"You *think* you did, or *did* you?" he asked insipidly, already knowing the answer. "Let me take a look. I'll have to idle over there." He gestured toward a serene cove. "I'll get out and see if I can figure this out." Chris is incredibly resourceful and can find calm in even the most chaotic moments. I was certain that he could remedy this problem quickly.

"Open the hatch and let's take a look in the battery compartment," Chris said. Once I opened the hatch, it became clear that this was no ordinary machine malfunction.

"Chris, there's a big *crack* in the boat," I said tepidly, unsure what to make of this development. He lifted himself up from the water, looked in, and immediately slipped back down. "Let's call Fort Myers Marine," I said peevishly.

I quickly dialed the number. "Hi, Colinda. This is Judy Weston, and we have a problem. I was wondering if there was anybody we could speak to regarding our power pole?" I chirped happily into my phone, as if I were picking flowers in some lovely meadow and not stranded in the bay, watching the rising water devour my husband.

"Sure, I'll get Chuck," she replied back, just as cheery. I handed the phone to Chris, who was now wading in chest-deep water, trying his best to wiggle and jiggle at the pole with one hand and hold the phone to his ear with the other. Anna began to pass the time by sunbathing on the deck, unaware of the severity of our trouble, while I stared impassively toward the horizon.

"Hi, Chuck," I could hear Chris say, "I got a problem with the shallow anchor." He waved his one arm wildly, like a maestro on steroids.

"Try cutting the hydraulic lines," I heard Chuck's commanding voice say with a strong sense of seriousness. There were a few more directions that I couldn't quite catch, but the phone call ended, and, by the look on Chris's face, so did the hope of leaving this place with a working shallow anchor. I became despondent as I looked toward my husband, who looked so strong in those glimmering waters. I knew danger was lurking; I just couldn't see it.

"Honey, please hurry and get in the boat. A shark is going to *eat* you!" I cried out.

"I am not going to be *eaten* by a shark!" he replied. He pulled his muscular body up onto the gunnels and into the boat. "We're going back to the ramp with the anchor in the down position," he said with a heavy dose of annoyance.

The plan was to head for the deep channel and take the Gulf back to the ramp while I held a rope that we'd tied around the broken anchor to give it a lift. "We'll take it slow," Chris said. "Hold the rope tight, and keep it lifted as much as you can." Anna, meanwhile, was somewhat oblivious to the fact that we had a crack in the stern that threatened to allow the Gulf of Mexico into our vessel. I didn't want to sully this afternoon unnecessarily with such unpleasant details. I was mentally making survival plans just in case. I figured if we took on water, I would have time to toss a life jacket to everyone and finish my half-eaten peanut-butter sandwich by the time the Gulf swallowed us up.

"Anna, are you OK?" I yelled over the engine.

"Yeah, this is great!" she exclaimed, throwing back her head into the wind.

"Ah, nice," I replied happily. I envisioned myself swimming next to her, with Chris behind us, as we made our way toward the mangroves that were about three miles away. If there were any sharks, they'd have to get to Chris and me first.

"Hey, there it is!" Chris yelled. We collectively sighed at the sight of Coon Key. "I'll get the truck. You take the helm." I released the rope from my reddened hands, as the shallow anchor continued to errantly weave about in the water. "OK, pull the boat up," Chris yelled from the dock, and I drove the wounded Redfisher up on the trailer. The sound of the pole scraping the concrete was like fingernails on a chalkboard.

"Ah, that's loud!" I shrieked. I noticed a small trail coming from our retreat.

"It didn't gouge the road. It just left a mark," Chris said assuredly.

After analyzing the situation and weighing out his options, Chris decided to use his hacksaw to cut the dangling pole in two, unbolt the frame, and toss the whole wet, inoperable anchor into the back of the truck. "We'll make an appointment with Fort Myers Marine tomorrow," Chris piped up. "Chuck will do us right."

"Yeah, after the repair I'm calling our shallow anchor The Shallamo," I stated plainly.

"Shallamo?" Chris repeated.

"Yeah, I'm placing a sticker prominently above our control button that reads *Remember the Shallamo*! That should keep our attention."

CHAPTER 11

The Good, The Bad, and the Itchy

THE FIRST DAY after our hiatus from the water was brutal. Chris and I hadn't been out for some time, and it appeared that I had forgotten a few details, such as bringing along a long-sleeved shirt, pants, and plenty of bug repellent. We took a short ride but didn't fish; we just wanted to get in and take a quick spin before sunset. My lack of planning proved to be a problem, and before going to bed that night, I grabbed a bottle for some solace. That bottle was at my side the entire evening, yet it did not provide me with the comfort I had hoped for. I finished the pink liquid and waited to start feeling something other than pain. I itched, scratched, fanned, and itched some more. I held cold compresses against the welts on my skin, hoping to stop the reaction from the deerfly bites I had acquired earlier. Applying the last drops of the calamine to my skin, I managed to stain my sheets and my pajama bottoms. That was it. Tossing the empty container aside around midnight, I tried my best to block out the torture.

The next morning I dressed more for the occasion and loaded the cooler. Our day started off pretty well. We were ready to cast our lines in and get reacquainted with the area that we had grown to respect. The mangroves, birds, and clouds drifted over us and greeted our presence with what felt like reverence. We had stopped at one of our tried-and-true holes, and it was there I realized that my leader line was frayed.

I sat on the gunnels and prepared to rig. I gathered the necessary items: a swivel, a weight, a hook, and a new leader line. I held the weight in my hand and grasped the fishing line. Suddenly a sense of unfamiliarity swept over me. *What do I do with this? Where does this go again?* I tried my best not to get overly upset about it, but time continued to drift by like those puffy clouds over my head, which were now creating strange patterns on the boat as they passed.

I became frustrated and yelled toward Chris, "I can't remember how to do this. Can you help me?" I really didn't like what this lapse implied.

"What do you *mean*, you can't rig your line?" he replied.

"I can't rig. I forgot how!" I yelled, and I thrust my rod toward him.

"Honey, you might have memory problems," he said with concern.

"I don't have a memory problem. I just forgot!" I insisted.

"OK, you go like this, and you twist that, and that's how you do it." He gently chose his words. He could see that I wasn't very happy that the swarming, biting flies had discovered my uncovered flesh and were making me part of the food chain. "OK, you wrap this around and tie this like this, and you're done," he repeated. He moved to the bow of the boat and proceeded to throw his line without a care in the world.

Our flats boat was performing well, taking the choppy Gulf waters like an experienced rodeo roughrider. I, on the other hand, continued to bounce around. I tried my best to hang on to a rod holder, the only tangible thing I could find. My grip was challenged by the troublesome waves that continued their whitecap display of power. *I should've sat back with Chris*, I thought as I continued to be jostled about. I found out pretty quickly that the cooler seat up front is not the best option in rough waters.

There was no point in trying to yell over the engine, so I threw up one arm and wiggled my hand as if to say, "Helloooooo! Can we turn at the next mangrove island, maybe?" Chris slowed the engine, causing the rushing cold water to slosh over the gunnels and douse me good. "Argh, that's cold," I yelled impetuously.

"You OK, honey?" Chris called from the captain's chair.

"Yeah, I'm fine. About how much longer until we get somewhere?" I inquired with a level of civility.

"Oh, not long at all," he said. He pushed the throttle forward.

Ugh, why does he have to be so ambiguous? I thought, wiping my face with a fish rag.

As we approached the backcountry, I was relieved to see that the surface of the water had become a gentle, soft ripple. I was instantly calmed, even though I knew that at some point we would have to venture back out into the Gulf. The winds have a tendency to pick up in the late afternoon, but I wasn't going to worry about that just then. I dismissed the images of swollen waves from my thoughts and stared straight ahead at the point we were approaching.

The tide was gently brushing up against the banks, where aging branches jutted out of the water, looking more like forgotten road rhubarb rusting in the afternoon sun. "This looks good," Chris said matter-of-factly. "We can use the shallow anchor."

That was music to my ears: I wouldn't have to crawl over to the small hatch, dig through a mountain of unorganized bags, find the metal anchor, and toss it over at the most advantageous time. There's not a lot of maneuvering for your hands as you whip the rope around in a figure eight when your cleat is nestled against the propellers of the trolling motor, and if you have a strong current tugging your line, you could end up losing your rope and anchor altogether. The current takes what it wants when it wants, especially if you are weak, timid, or hesitant.

As fate would have it, our supersecret spots were fairly slow. Chris managed to hook a few mangrove snapper, and I continued catching inanimate objects, such as broken oyster shells and tree branches. "Chris, I'm stuck," I moaned. I yanked at my line, which was now wrapped around a tree branch. "Can you help, pleeeeeeease?"

"OK, just let me finish this cast," he said, bristled by the fact that I was annoying him. Once he got a nibble, he began talking to himself in a whisper. "Come back for another bite...oh...oooh bite...bite...bite." Suddenly his line yanked upward. "Damn, I missed." He grunted in disappointment. "OK, where exactly are you stuck?" I gave my rod a small yank, and we pinpointed the area where my line was being held hostage by the branches of a mangrove.

I stood on the bow as we slowly approached the tree. I was able to unwind the line and release the hook just in time. "OK, I got it!" I said. And with that he backed slowly away, avoiding a collision with a well-rooted tree. To ensure safety for the wildlife, we're adamant about retrieving monofilament or any other angler debris from trees, and we often make it a point to stop if we notice any forgotten lines hanging from branches and dispose of them in our trash container.

Chris steered the boat northeast, heading for Fakahatchee Bay, where we thought the fishing might be a little better. There's a place close to the bay that has proven itself a real sweet spot for snapper on the outgoing tide, so we were naturally relieved to see that there was no one anchored up. As we readied our lines, a large boat approached, stopping abruptly. The captain stood up in his chair, gave a look in our direction, and made a drastic turn, leaving us bobbing in its wake. You could tell just by the way the boat turned and kicked up water that the captain was annoyed. "He was a guide," Chris said, smiling, "but we were here first." He threw out his line into the bay.

My dismal showing continued, while Chris kept reeling them in. "Throw over there, honey. That's where they are," he said, making a gesture toward the fallen branches that stuck out from the water's edge. As I tried to explain to him that the spot he was showing me was the spot I was trying, his line tightened. When it's time to reel in a big one, it doesn't matter who has it on the line! Chris stood steadfastly as the drag from his reel let out a short scream. This was followed by silence, a longer scream, and silence again. "OK, come over here. He's moving this way." He gestured with his leg to show me the way. I lunged forward, watching as the line moved from left to right and then circled around and repeated. It was as if the fish had become disoriented.

"What is it?" I asked, almost breathless.

"I don't know!" Chris replied. He held his line tight. It was anyone's guess, and until he could get it to the surface, we were left to fight an unseen opponent. By now Chris had the upper hand, and up through the swarthy waters came a glimmer of what was on the line. "It's a black drum. OK, he's almost ready!" Chris said. "OK—now!" I dipped the net in, and the fish strongly swished away. I missed!

The sound of an engine came up, and it was then that my perfect fantasy was about to happen. I've daydreamed about having a big fish on the line when fishermen suddenly appear from nowhere and watch me with envious eyes as I reel it in. *Yes, look at me! I am the greatest! I am skillful! I am woman!* But it was Chris who had the fish, and this was no fantasy. This was real! I leaned over, and this time I scooped the black drum up out of the water.

"Wow! Look at it," Chris yelled. With that he hoisted the fish skyward, and the waters from Fakahatchee Bay dripped from the fish and onto his sunburned forehead, anointing him. The fishermen in the other boat applauded loudly, whistled, and then immediately marked the spot on their GPS. I had to laugh.

Later that evening, I continued to nurse my deerfly bites, which now looked like diner pancakes. I'd tried cactus gel, Bactine, Cortizone 10, plain cortisone, After Bite, mushy baking powder, and some healing balm I bought at the flea market, but nothing worked! "I'm glad this kind of thing didn't happen when I first started fishing," I said to Chris, who wasn't paying much attention. "I might not have wanted to continue."

"What did you say?" he asked casually.

"Oh, never mind," I replied with annoyance. "Just try to help me remember the bug spray next time, OK?" I soaked some rags in cold water and formed compresses against my skin. *This will do,* I said to myself. *It's all part of fishing—the good, the bad, and the itchy.*

CHAPTER 12

Texan-Sized River

"Carpe diem," I whispered. I rolled off of the pull-out bed in our fifth-wheel camper, tucked away at our campsite in Chokoloskee, Florida. Today was the day we were headed for Houston River! I'd seen the mouth of this Texan-sized waterway, and I grew even more energetic considering that the weather was delightful.

After breakfast it was time to head over to the bait shop in Everglades City. Fishermen who had signed up for a tournament were milling about and talking among themselves. The top prize would be bestowed upon the angler who could catch the redfish that had a special tag attached to its scaly red body. I had noticed the boat ramp the day before and wondered why all those men dressed in their fishing finery looked so determined.

It was time to pay for our shrimp, and Chris suggested I look at lures. *Oh gosh no*, I thought. Shopping for lures and jigs is a lot like shopping for mascara to me: I get so confused! The young man at the counter was making it easy for me. He presented a lure that would nearly guarantee a hit every time. He dangled the rubbery form of a squiggly shrimp, complete with a movable tail, in front of my eyes. "Hmmm, looks interesting," I commented, only half-interested. Chris was intrigued and asked a few more questions about this particular lure. Then he suggested we walk over to the wall of angler ammunition.

Chris strolled over and plucked one from the hook. "Look—a root-beer shrimp."

"Wow, I didn't know that fish liked root beer–flavored shrimp. That's cool! Root beer–flavored shrimp—who knew?" I said loudly. By now the clerk's face had turned a slight shade of red, and it appeared he was on the brink of a full-blown laugh.

"Uh, honey, no, its root beer–*colored*. They don't make root beer–flavored shrimp," Chris said gently. It occurred to me in a matter of seconds what I had done. The way Chris was looking at me seemed to say, "You're showing your girlishness." *Oh God, what do I do?* I thought quickly. I looked at the young man, who was doing his best to retain a respectable composure, and I laughed.

"Yeah, isn't that crazy," I said, trying to deflect my faux pas, "a fish-loving, root beer–flavored shrimp!" There was no laughter, and Chris immediately changed the subject.

We drove southward and crossed the small bridge that leads to Chokoloskee. I could see the tide, and I didn't like the conditions. "Well, how low can it go?" I asked playfully. You could practically walk across the bay due to the low tide, and that wasn't what I wanted to see. From our dock, it was pretty apparent that the only place we were going was back to camp. Our Redfisher 16 was stuck in the muck of the tiny canal that led to the bay. There was no moving this boat, and the only things that seemed to be alive were the pesky deerflies that circled my leg, waiting to harpoon me at any moment.

"Let's go back to camp," Chris said with reservation. That wasn't the news I wanted. I was all dressed up (if you consider shorts and a tank top dressed up) and had nowhere to go, but I had to adhere to the captain's wishes. Chris pointed out that it would be pretty stupid and unsafe to try to cross the bay at such a time. Showing my discontent, I sulked all the way back to camp. "Go on a bike ride," Chris said, his voice lifting with encouragement.

"OK," I said. I grabbed my headphones, turned up my tunes, and took off.

My bike is blue and has a nifty basket attached to it. Oftentimes I find usable items along the road, such as my most recent acquisition—a flotation cushion. As I pedaled farther, I noticed a truck heading my way pulling a nice-looking boat. As it passed me, an unidentifiable object flew right at my face. I ducked in time, and when I opened my eyes, I saw a black hat still turning circles along the side of the road. Intrigued, I pedaled over and discovered that it was probably new. It had some embroidered words touting an alcoholic beverage and a detailed emblem. I sat on my bike, thinking the boater would turn around and claim his hat, but after a few minutes of dead air, I decided to resume my biking and head on in with a new hat and a new flotation device.

I turned back toward Chokoloskee and pedaled by the Havana Café, wishing for the place to be open. It had closed for the season, and I was missing the affable staff and the smell of fresh garlic wafting in the air. *By now the tide should have come up enough*, I thought, and I headed back to camp, where Chris was trimming a few hedges.

"Let's check out the water and see if we can go," I said.

"OK, let's go," Chris said, putting his trimmers down. It appeared that the waterline had risen enough, and we readied our boat for the journey toward Houston River.

I hurried Chris along; his movements seemed sloth-like. I figured he was trying to stall our departure because he knew in his salty heart that the journey would present problems. "Why did we buy a flats boat if we were going to worry about a little shallow water?" I asked.

"Honey, just because we have a flats boat doesn't mean we can boat across mud. Even if we can get it on a plane, we could end up getting stuck. But OK, we'll go."

The easterly gusts of wind blew hard. It appeared as if it were pushing the water back out to the Gulf even though it was time for the tide to turn inward. "It sure is breezy," I chimed happily.

Chris did his best to continue his pleasant demeanor. "Yep, sure is," he agreed. We whizzed through Crooked Creek, steering clear of the banks that were bone dry.

"I can't wait to get to Houston!" I yelled. "We've got plenty of shrimp—" Suddenly I had an awful thought. "Oh gosh, I forgot the shrimp! Chris, we're going to have to go back."

"Oh no!" Chris moaned in disbelief. "We'll just keep going and use lures."

"Heck no," I said. "I'm not going to Houston for the first time and not having shrimp. Let's go back!"

"OK," he replied, and with that we circled around and went back to camp.

Our second departure was a lot like the first, but we had a little more urgency to our speed. The tide was up nicely, and we whizzed our way through

Lopez River, Crooked Creek, and several other bays until we saw the mouth of Houston River. I had a renewed love for fishing that day, and I was trying my best to forget about the last few outings. I had a new Penn reel that felt and sounded as smooth as a Miles Davis record, and I anticipated the strength of fighting snook leaping in the air and falling back into the cool waters. I smiled toward my candy-apple-red reel, which I had just recently learned was a Fierce Penn reel.

Until recently, I hadn't been aware that there were *types* of Penn reels. I was brazen enough to start talking fishing equipment with a charter fisherman who also sold angling equipment on the side. "I just love my Penn reel!" I told him.

"Oh, what kind do you have?" he asked.

Oops, I'm busted, I thought. "Um, I didn't know there were any different kinds," I sheepishly said.

"Sure there are. Can you describe your reel?"

"Well, it's lined in candy-apple-red coloring, and—"

"Oh, I know which one you have," he interjected. And with that he pulled out from the counter the exact reel that I own. "You have a Fierce," he said, smiling.

"Oh yeah, I'm *fierce*, and I have the reel to back that up!" I laughed and then promptly left.

Houston River was wide and bustling. Everything seemed so animated. The birds were soaring, the trees were swaying, and the water seemed to caress the banks as we carefully idled nearby. I peered into the water at my reflection as it bounced and twisted, and I felt like I was seeing my distorted self in a fun-house mirror.

"Where are we going first?" I asked.

"Well, I just don't know," Chris said. "This is all just guessing." By this time, I had come to understand what to look for when judging a potential fishing hole, and as the boat began to stop, I looked over and saw what appeared to be an excellent choice. The current was moving against the point, there seemed to be some structure (fish hide around structures), and there were some branches that were partly submerged. Perfect!

Casting in the wind is about as easy as flying a kite on a windless day. To improve the length of my cast, I added a heavier sinker on my line. I kept casting and reeling back in, and suddenly the fish arrived. We were catching and releasing dozens of mangrove snapper. It seemed to go in cycles: the fish appeared and then disappeared; the fish appeared and then disappeared.

"Hey, let's go to another spot," Chris said. He upped the shallow anchor, and we were once again scanning the shoreline, seeking something that *felt* right.

Land hunters have the distinct advantage of seeing their prey and focusing on a tangible target, whereas fishermen use their instinctual insight. Think like a fish. Be fishlike. Get in the mind of a fish. Become a fish. If you want to hook a fish, you have to *understand* a fish. Even if you do all these things and have all the necessary gear, this does not always translate into hooking the fish you want. But sometimes it does. Insight and visual sight are both invaluable to any hunter, and a little luck sure helps.

Chris found a lively area just west of our other spot, where pods of bait seemed to be dancing on the surface. "Hey, look, Chris—bait! And where there's bait, there's a predator!" I said. I cast my line near the activity. It didn't take long for my line to jerk strongly and take off. "I got something!" I yelled. My reel whizzed, taking out some drag. I popped my tip up, setting the hook, and with that a large snook surprised me, leaping from the water like a jack-in-the-box. Surprise! I yanked my tip up, trying to hold on as I watched my line head for the bank. "He's heading into the branches," I said, and with that I held tight.

"Do I get the net?" Chris yelled.

"Yeah," I breathlessly whispered. "I think so!"

Snook are revered among sportsmen and are arguably the most fiercely focused species I've encountered. They have all the attributes of a champion NASCAR driver: they're focused, polished, and determined. They also can take tight turns at mind-blowing speeds. Their sleek physiques are detailed with custom go-faster racing stripes along the side, and they always seem camera-ready, even after a hard-fought fight. Good-looking in a humble way, snook are less intimidating than some of the other fighters partly because of their gummy mouth.

After I was able to get the fish to the gunnels, we took a quick photo and placed the fish back in the water, where it quickly disappeared. "Good-bye, Mario. And good luck," I said. Chris and I have fun bestowing names on the fish we place back in the water. Dale, Martin, Danica, and even Shirley are fitting names for any snook. Sadly, there are probably more race-car-driver names out there than there are snook, due to overfishing and a severe cold snap in 2010 that decimated the population. Currently there are strict rules regarding the harvesting of the species, and if you are brazen enough to disregard the law and you get caught, you will be handed a stiff penalty and possibly lose your boat. When we enter snook season, I know I won't harvest a single one, even if I am lucky enough to hook a keeper. I'm sure they're delicious, but so are snapper, trout, and mackerel. I'm just not that interested in eating one. Let them drive on, and may they never see that checkered flag shaped like a frying pan.

The late-afternoon sky had crept over the top of the mangrove trees that had provided us with shade and solace from the spring winds, and we pulled anchor and headed back to camp.

"I just love Houston and can't wait to come back!" I yelled over the roar of the engine. Chris just smiled. He popped the top of a cold beer and settled in his chair, where he tweaked the GPS. We entered the canal that leads to the dock, and I noticed that there was nobody around. *Great, no audience this time*, I thought. I turned to Chris and asked if I could dock the boat. The winds were still strong, but I really wanted to learn how to ease my boat into her slip.

"OK," Chris said. "But take your time."

I grabbed the wheel and began my turn. "This is what it must feel like if you drive on ice," I whispered. There are no brakes, and control is nearly impossible. Somehow I made it through the poles, but it went downhill from there.

"Watch out!" Chris yelled, and just as he finished his sentence, I crashed into the dock, causing it to crack.

"Oops!" I nonchalantly said. The damage was done, and there was not a thing I could do about it, so why get bent out of shape?

"Honey, you could have broken the trolling motor!" Chris said. His tone was distinctly disappointed.

"Well, that didn't get damaged—the dock did," I said in my defense.

"I'm not sure you're ready to do this again anytime soon," he said flatly.

"Well, I have to do it. How else am I supposed to get better at it if I don't do it?" I was resolute.

"OK, well, next time be more careful."

"Yeah, sure," I laughed. I climbed the ladder to solid ground. I'd been to Houston, and there was nothing that could upset me at that moment, not even a cracked dock or a flustered husband.

CHAPTER 13

— ❦ —

Finding the *S* Curve

THE DAY WAS all wrong: the tide, my casting, the water levels, the temperature—you name it. I realize every fishing trip won't produce a cache, but I refused to budge from my smugness. By the time we got to West Pass, I was pretty much through with our day before it had even had a chance to begin.

Chris, ever the optimist, anchored without delay at every spot he knew would offer us a potential catch. He gleefully stood on the bow, basking in all his glory and relishing the idea that he would hook a big one. He was undaunted. He was confident. He was happy. I was not.

"Oh no, another catfish," he would yell from the bow. Meanwhile, I was catching tree limbs and various other inanimate objects that found their way around my useless hook.

"I hate fishing," I flatly stated.

Chris did not respond. After a few minutes, he looked in my direction and said, "You need to adjust your attitude." Then he calmly returned to his casting.

There it was. An affirmation so glaring it was as blinding as the sun's reflection. It crackled like Fourth of July sparklers on the water's surface. *You need to adjust your attitude* kept swirling in my mind like a raging whirlpool, circling and circling, trying to suck me deeper into the depths of my lousy demeanor. *OK*, I thought, *how can I turn this around? I have to get busy doing something other than hooking hardheaded catfish.* I reached for the scrub brush, doused it with river water, and began cleaning the deck. A sense of accomplishment washed over me as the dark mud rolled away with every brisk swish of my brush, leaving the deck as pristine as ever.

I began to think positive thoughts and started questioning my behavior. *Why am I being so obstinate? Why am I being unappreciative?* To make matters worse, I had earlier hooked a nice fish and wrestled it to the gunnels, only to find out that it was a gag grouper.

"Nice fish," Chris shouted enthusiastically, encouraging me.

"It's only an undersized gag grouper. It doesn't count," I replied. I took the hook from its lip and tossed it unceremoniously back into the calm waters. I hadn't even bothered to admire its beauty. *I am not appreciating these gifts that are right here in front of me.* It was as if I had the best seat in the house at a fine stage production and I wasn't paying any attention.

"Hey, honey, do you want to try a popping cork?" Chris asked, jarring me loose from my soul-searching.

"Sure!" I yelled. I jumped from my seat, reaching for the rod he had thrust in my direction. I was starving for some mental deflection, so I devoured his suggestion. "OK, now refresh my memory—how do you cast with a cork?" I had fished with a cork about a year earlier, but hadn't given it any more thought since.

"You toss it near the bank, but don't throw it in the trees," he said. "When you see the bobber sink, set your hook." *Sounds easy enough*, I thought, and with a big, arching cast, up the bobber went into the air as the shrimp on the hook soared in a circular motion before hitting the water and disappearing. When using a bobber, you are less likely to catch catfish—or so I thought. After a few moments, the bobber did indeed go under. I set the hook and reeled in a rather large-sail catfish.

"Ugh! Another catfish!" I said with a laugh.

Fishing with a bobber is more demanding than it seems. First of all, you have to keep a good eye on your bobber, something that was difficult for me, considering I am easily distracted by such things as passing fishermen, the spouting sounds of dolphins in the distance, birds singing, and the constant swatting of horseflies, mosquitoes, and various other biting insects that frequent the backcountry.

"Are you watching your bobber, honey?" Chris yelled as he continued his casting.

"Um, yeah, but it's not doing anything but bobbing around," I replied humorously. I was feeling relieved that my spirits had lifted, even though we continued to catch catfish.

"I think it's time to go back," Chris said, and he reeled in.

Just when I was starting to have a little fun, we're leaving! I thought. But the captain knows best. And as late afternoon approaches, he takes serious note of such things as the tides, the winds, and how many beers are left in the cooler.

"I want to find the *S* curve that will take us back to Chokoloskee," Chris said, fidgeting with the GPS.

"Why?" I asked. "Why can't we just take the Gulf?"

"Because I want to know," he replied. "Relax and let me look at the map." After several long minutes, he motored southward, made a few turns around several islands, and declared triumphantly, "Here it is—the *S* curve!" We roared on, basking in the carefreeness of the exploration, and before we knew it, Chokoloskee appeared between a pair of matching islands.

"Wow, that *was* quick," I yelled over the engine. We began to slow as we entered the bay, where a line of canoers had paused. Their heads were all bowed as if in prayer, but upon closer inspection, I noticed that they were all busy texting. "I don't understand why anyone would be texting sitting in a canoe in the middle of utopia. It just doesn't make sense," I said to Chris, who nodded in agreement. We didn't bother waving toward them; they wouldn't have noticed anyway.

Chris made the turn into the small canal that led to the ramp. We were greeted by a man who looked over at us and heartily declared, "Hey, you brought her back after all!"

His laughter subsided, and I looked over to him and yelled right back, "I'm a keeper, you know!"

"I bet you are," he said, and he continued walking the dock.

"Chris, why do you think he said that?" I asked.

"I don't know," he said. He jostled the boat into the small sliver of a dock space that we own. "I'll get the truck," he said. He leaped onto the dock and headed toward camp. I began to worry. There were several fishermen at the fillet station, and that meant only one thing: I'd have an audience when pulling the boat up on the trailer. Normally this would not be a problem, but this dock space was about as big as an office cubicle.

Chris returned and gave me a what-are-you-waiting-for look that caused my cheeks to become even redder than they had been just a few minutes before. I was afraid of what I knew could possibly happen. *I am about to give girls a bad name*, I thought as I teetered between pride and a full-blown retreat. As I pondered my options, Chris walked over.

"What's the holdup?" he asked.

"I can't do this." I whispered so as to not tip off the men who were eyeing me from the fillet station.

"Do what, honey? Back the boat up?" Chris asked, puzzled by my apparent dilemma. "Yes you can. Just take it slow, OK?" I took a deep breath, and in a moment of chivalry, I rallied my inner self and let go of the dock rope. *There is no turning back now. I have committed myself to the challenge.*

I was sitting rather tall at the helm, grasping the throttle with my slender girl hands and hoping this wouldn't look like a bad bumper-car ride. There were boats to the left and right and in back of me, all neatly tied up and softly swaying with the rippling water. I calculated my move with the understanding that my boat had no breaks and that with inertia a movement can't be retracted. I gently prodded the throttle, budging backward ever so slightly. *Here we go*, I thought, trying hard to breathe normally, channeling my inner strong girl. I could sense the eyes following me, the lions crouched in the bushes, waiting to pounce.

A sudden burst of confidence exploded within me, destroying any self-doubt. I glided our boat backward without hitting anybody or anything.

"OK!" Chris yelled from the ramp, "bring her in!" I happily looked for the uprights on the trailer, and within minutes I had the boat up against the winch.

"Hey, you did pretty good," the fishermen all quipped in unison. I smiled and basked in my victorious moment—only to have it shattered in seconds: the boat slipped off backward and into the muddy water.

"Honey, give it more throttle, and keep the engine going forward."

"What are you talking about?" I snapped. I did my best not to run into anything or anybody. The boat was swaying back and forth, and my confidence was waning.

By now my adoring crowd had diverted their eyes and gone back to the business of filleting their fish. "Give it more throttle, and keep giving it gas as you hit the winch!"

"Okay," I whispered, somewhat angry but determined. I wasn't sure why this was happening, since I'd never had to perform this maneuver before. I pushed the throttle forward, and *bang!* I hit the winch and kept gassing it. The engine churned so loudly I had the crowd cringing.

"OK, OK!" Chris yelled, "We got it hooked!" Upon closer inspection, Chris lamented that I had brought it in crooked. "Well, it'll do. It's not pretty, but it's on."

"I'm not perfect," I said as we headed to our camp, "but I'm a keeper, right, honey?"

"That's right," he replied, and he flashed a smile worth remembering.

CHAPTER 14

The White Rainbow (Fog Bow)

THE MORNING MOVED in slowly. I sensed its arrival, tossed my covers onto the floor, and looked out into the new day. To my surprise, a heavy fog crept eerily across the bay, coloring it a dirty gray that resembled a mound of forgotten city snow. I furrowed my brow in discontent, trying my hardest to think that my eyes were deceiving me. *What is this? And where is the blue sky?* I wasn't ready to be surprised by anything or anybody. I wanted a blue sky filled with warmth and promise; instead it appeared that we would be boating in a slushy pile of half-melted snow.

"Hey Chris, I can't really see anything. Are we still going fishing?" I asked.

"We'll see," he replied, a tinge of concern in his voice.

Our arrival at the dock confirmed my misgivings: a thick patch of sea fog continued to sneak over the bay. I was headstrong and determined to go fishing; Chris was more reluctant. After a brief discussion, I persuaded him that the fog would probably lift soon, and we launched the boat into the motionless water. Chris idled cautiously, and we made our way into Chokoloskee Bay, where we were abruptly confronted with a haunting landscape. Dark shadows appeared randomly, and the inauspicious air had hushed the clarion calls of the waterbirds above. The unstable mood consumed our boat, and a rumination tugged at my intuition, urging me to turn around.

"Do you think this will *lift* soon?" I asked.

"Well, maybe," Chris said. He scratched at his chin. By that time I was certain that, at any moment, Charon, the ferryman to Hades, would emerge from the shrouded banks and extend his icy fingers toward us, demanding payment.

With each passing moment, one fact was clear: we couldn't see *anything*. Chris idled along and managed to find shelter in a small cove. It seemed safe, and it offered us a respite from our situation. We huddled together, making our game plan. Chris suggested that we head out toward the Gulf, and I nodded in approval even as I gazed into the gray void that awaited us. "Yeah, let's go to the Gulf. I bet it's clear there," I said. Yet a feeling of apprehension swept over me.

As we left the safety of the cove, I realized I had left something else there—my enthusiasm for the adventure. Every point of reference faded away with each forward chug of our engine, and I became disoriented. We monitored our manual compass and inched our way westward. Slowly the shadows of the landscape dissolved into the mist, indicating the presence of the Gulf of Mexico.

"Did we make it?" I whispered.

"Yeah, I think so," Chris replied, unfazed by our situation. We headed southeast. By now the only things audible were the sputtering engine and the lonesome tinging sounds of an eerie, damp wind.

Fear is not necessarily what I felt. There was no time for that. Instead I knelt on the bow and *listened*.

"What are you doing, honey?"

"Ssh, *quiet*," I pleaded. "I'm trying to hear for any engine sounds or whatever." Chris seemed amused at my antics and stared at me through his moistened glasses, as if I were the entertainment portion of this adventure.

"There's nobody out here. Relax!" he said, shaking his head.

"We're out here. And if we're out here, somebody else is, too!" I shouted back, annoyed at the fact that he didn't have a care in the world, and I was on the brink of a full-blown panic attack. Our small vessel was not equipped with fog lights, just a tiny navigational light that would be the equivalent of using a small candle in a large, dark cave.

"Chris, I can't see *anything*. Do you think someone will crash into us?" I asked casually, but I was profoundly paranoid.

"No, honey. This is a big Gulf. There's no way someone will be crashing into us." He was impassive. *We are not lost. We know where we are.* These two (factual) thoughts offered me little comfort as the sea fog continued to consume us. I blinked my eyes slowly and surrendered to our predicament. There was nothing left to do but wait.

We came across a hint of a landscape that looked more like a mystical beast as we idled past the jagged silhouette of the islands. I found comfort in knowing that the shoreline wasn't far, that if it came down to it, I could swim to safety along the banks of the mangroves. As we motored forward, there seemed to be a break in the mist, and we could begin to see about twenty yards in front of us.

"Hey! Blue sky, straight ahead!" Chris yelled. "Thank goodness." He dried his glasses with a fish rag. Our stagnant demeanor grew optimistic as we continued south, leaving the gray prison behind us.

After nearly an hour spent blindly moving through the Gulf, the wind shifted and blue sky continued to peek through the remnants of the gray armor that had covered us. I leaned back on the console and looked upward, relishing the fact that I had weathered my fear. It was then that I noticed an auspicious vision above me.

"Look Chris, a *white* rainbow!" I yelled, pointing toward the west.

"Yeah, how about that. I've never seen a rainbow like that," he replied. He stretched his neck around to get a better view. I grabbed my camera and had Chris sit on the gunnel. I framed him perfectly, capturing the grandeur of the moment.

"Wow, I wonder if anybody else is noticing it," I said. That was definitely something special.

We arrived at Lostmans River shortly after observing the rainbow. The water had calmed, and the warm sunshine soothed me. Fatigued from our journey, I reached in the cooler for some water. "We'll head over there," Chris said, gesturing toward a bank where he'd fished before.

"OK, let's do it," I eagerly replied. I was ready to put the whole fog incident behind me. We dropped anchor, and I began baiting my hook. Just then another boater came too close, causing a wake and jarring our anchor loose. "Why doesn't he slow down?" I said, annoyed. I placed my rod down so I could reposition our anchor. Chris paid no attention to me. He was busy catching fish. I was fortunate enough to see a stingray project itself toward the sky as I continued my task with the anchor, and manatees drifted alongside our boat, intermittently sticking their nostrils out to breathe in the air. It was a busy river, and that day everything felt alive and free.

"OK, let's try that area over there," Chris said, and he readied the boat for departure. Fishing requires strategy. It's not guesswork but more of a feeling. Chris has that instinctual knack to find fish, and he guided us toward an area with a deep hole, where bigger fish might be hanging out. "This could be good," Chris said, handing me my rod. I baited my hook, cast toward the hole, and counted to sixteen. I tightened my line and waited. *Zing!* My reel started burning.

"Chris, I got a big one, I think!"

"OK, honey. Reel it in!" he yelled. "Reel it in!"

I held my rod steady as I began a tug-of-war with a fish, and it seemed that I was on the losing side. Many thoughts ran through my mind as I held steady. *Did I check my drag? Was my leader line frayed? Do I let it run, or do I continue to reel in? Will my reel stick? Did I check to make sure my reel was secure on my rod?* All these questions were, of course, too late, considering I had a large fish on my hook. I remained calm and briefly closed my eyes, trying to visualize what the fish was doing. I reacted accordingly by lifting my rod and keeping my line tight. With an ever-so-gentle circular motion, I reeled in, keeping strong.

"Tip up!" Chris yelled, breaking my train of thought. Within minutes a large gray fish appeared. "It's a drum!" Chris yelled. He reached for the net, and with one quick dip, he scooped up the fish and placed it on the deck. We immediately measured the black drum and found that it indeed was slot size. "Keeper!" Chris yelled, placing it in the live well. "Nice job, honey!" he added as he closed the lid.

The afternoon sun was now commanding my attention. It was too late for sunscreen; the damage was done. I could see my distorted reflection in the metal rod holder, and I noticed that my face had a ruddy color that looked odd when I took my sunglasses off. The tide was coming in so strong that it looked like it might take out a few trees with it.

"There will probably be sheepshead here and possibly other species," Chris said. He lowered the shallow-water anchor. "We better start casting before it gets too deep." We baited our hooks and started casting toward the banks, and things began to get interesting.

Every cast came back with a sizeable sheepshead, biting hard. "Hurry, Chris! I have a big one, get the net," I grunted. After a few attempts, we finally got the feisty fish aboard. It was flopping and flipping its tail, and it watched every move I made when I came close.

"OK, honey. You got it from here. I'm going back to fishing," Chris said. He picked up his rod and headed for the bow. Our small deck really made this sheepshead look big, and I approached it with caution. As I slowly bent down to pick it up, the fish jumped at me as if it were throwing punches. Its angry eyes were intimidating, and I hastily retreated to the stern.

"Chris, can you help me?" I asked in a whinesome tone.

"You can do it. Keep trying."

"I caaaaan't."

"Yes, you can!"

"This fish is mean, and I can't get the hook out. Will you help me—*please*!" I pleaded. Reluctantly, Chris set his rod down, picked the fish up with no problem, and then flicked his wrist, releasing the hook.

"OK, here is your fish. Now put it in the live well," he said sternly. He handed over the fat fish with wide eyes that glared my way. I looked away as I held it tightly, and I could feel the fish relax. Little did I know that it was actually playing possum, a tactic I never thought a fish would think to use.

"Can you open the live well, Chris?" I asked.

"OK, but hurry up and put the fish in." As he opened the box, I dropped my catch in sideways instead of placing it in headfirst. It hit the water in the live well, and with the strength of ten fish, it willed itself upward while leaping out. It arched itself upward and over and into the rushing waters, where it paused on the water's surface but didn't dive downward. Instead it began skidding sideways like a pebble, skimming across the water's surface. All the way to the bank it went in that cartoonish way. I honestly thought it was going to climb a tree!

"Get back in this boat, fish!" I yelled, laughing.

"I've never seen a fish do that," Chris said. He scratched his head in disbelief.

The tide had slowed, and we decided to head home. We were still laughing about the sheepshead that got away as we glided through Lostmans River. "He's probably down there telling human stories to his friends," Chris joked.

"Yeah, what a story," I replied. I laughed heartily. We were riding high on the tide, and the sea fog had now become a faint memory.

CHAPTER 15

The She-Captain

With frothy clouds topping off the morning sky and the winds of March shaking the leaves of the mangroves like a tambourine, I knew the day would be full of promises. Some of those promises included (in no particular order) having a better attitude, helping with anchor-tossing duties, being a better friend to nature, releasing my own catfish, and wearing sunblock, to name a few. Feeling rather bold, I offered to back the boat off the trailer.

"OK, honey. I'll be right back. Just pull the boat into our dock space and wait there." Chris spoke calmly as he drove away to park the truck elsewhere.

"OK, I got this!" I yelled back. Perspiration began to form on my brow. There wasn't anybody at the dock when I took on this endeavor, but as Chris disappeared into the background, several fishermen appeared and were waiting to unload their boats into the tiny canal where I was floating.

"Is there a problem?" one of the fishermen asked as I sat in my boat. I wasn't exactly in trouble—more like somebody who couldn't navigate a boat into the tiny slip and had decided to drop the shallow-water anchor right in the middle of the canal instead. I decided to come clean.

"Well, I'm not the best when it comes to docking the boat," I sheepishly said to the young men who now were pacing along the dock in front of me.

At the time I thought honesty was the best policy. Besides, I couldn't come up with a believable lie. It was pretty obvious that I was a girl in a boat in the middle of the canal, sitting in the path of anglers who weren't sure how to approach the situation without offending me. Their rugged voices now blended like a barbershop quartet: "Throw us a rope," they chimed simultaneously.

"Oh, OK," I muttered, trying to lift my voice with some energetic cooperation. By now Chris had arrived.

"What are you *doing*, honey?" he asked in a singsong.

"Well, I...well...couldn't quite...well." My response seemed to skip like an old vinyl record.

"Bring the boat over here, and let me get on," Chris said, his voice firm but gentle. He waved toward me. The other men went about their business as if nothing had happened, but the smiles on their tanned faces began to grow like vines.

Once Chris took the helm, we puttered out of the canal and went at full throttle into Chokoloskee Bay. We glided as if we were on glass, slipping and sliding and turning and bending as the rushing water sprayed out from the stern like whipped cream from a can. In the blur of the moment, I glanced toward the shoreline. There, the mangroves appeared to be wearing red mustaches, while birds flew perpendicular against the water's edge, scraping their feathers against the emerald liquid. I mentally prepared my game plan. *Think. Stay focused. Take time to bait your hook properly. Check for frayed lines. Keep control as you cast. Have patience.* On this trip I really wanted to see a mangrove snapper that had some size. It had been a long time since Chris and I successfully found a spot that generated keeper-sized fish, but this day felt different. The sun caressed my shoulders, and the gentle wind was just strong enough to wrestle the mosquitoes off my skin before they had the chance to bother me.

Chris parked along a potential spot and eased the shallow anchor down. I have to admit I really like spots that are shallow-anchor friendly. It's less work for me: throwing the anchor down and yanking it back up gets a little labor-intensive at times. After the boat was anchored suitably, the tide tried its best to tug the anchor right out of its stronghold, but the anchor won out, and the waters rushed along our gunnels.

"Wow, this is a strong tide," Chris mentioned. He kept casting toward the bank, only to find that his line had been commandeered by the rushing waters, which sent it to the middle of Russell Key Channel. "I don't think our bait is even hitting the bottom," Chris exclaimed as he reeled back in. "Let's find another place."

I was surprised that we weren't catching anything in this rushing water that I was certain contained many fish. *They're probably racing through, hoping to make it alive to the next structure, where they can comfortably drift around the banks and try not to get eaten by anything while they look for someone to eat,* I thought, casting once again.

We decided to get out of the hasty waters of Russell Key Channel and find something a little less frantic. We idled around before deciding on a small cove where the mangroves were extra bushy. The sun-dappled leaves and soft winds provided a much-needed respite from the surge of energy that comes with a roaring incoming tide. "This looks good," Chris said, and he pushed the button that created a low roaring sound followed by a soft plunk from the shallow-water anchor. We were running low on shrimp, so Chris decided to throw his lure. I got to use the limp old shrimp that were left over from our last fishing trip. As part of my "good attitude" strategy, I decided to use the old shrimp and not complain about it.

I took the mushy meat and slowly worked it as best as I could along the shank of my hook, and then I threw my line toward the bank. If you don't thread the shrimp on just right, it will become an easy item to steal right off the hook! I was instantly amazed at the immediate strike and continued with a surprised excitement. One cast after another provided me with keeper-sized snapper. The fish were all hiding in one area just shy of the bank. If I threw too far to the right, no bites. Too far to the left, no bites. But when I threw right in the middle of a pair of fat mangroves, that proved to be *the* spot. My backhanded casting was as fierce as my precision, hitting my target every time. Chris was reeling them in as well, and he suggested that we mark the area on the GPS. "What do you want to name it?" he asked.

"I don't know, maybe Snapper Spot?" I replied. "I'm really not in the name-this-spot mode at the moment."

"No, not that," he laughed.

"I'm not that original," I replied under my breath. "Maybe March Madness?"

"Nah, let's just call it March, since the month is March," Chris said, and he plugged in the spot.

"We're almost out of shrimp," I said toward Chris, who continued using his favorite lure.

"OK, the rest is yours, honey."

Reaching into the small pile of squishy bait shrimp, I tried my best to find one suitable to thread along my eagle-claw hook. By now, most of the hooks in my tackle box were dulled from clanking around in the slots of the box. I tested a few of them by poking the barb into my thumb, and I couldn't even get blood. Squishy shrimp and dull hooks—not a combo you want while fishing. There was nothing left to do but fish on.

I hooked a clump of white meat that fluttered in the wind like a torn screen as I raised my rod in preparation for my last cast. *This will do.* I laughed to myself. *If I hook something with this, it'll be a miracle.* Taking aim I threw a backhanded cast that hit my target perfectly. After a few moments, there was a tug, and I instantly pulled my rod tip up.

"I got something—it's big!" I shouted. My clear monofilament line was headed toward the bank. Whatever was on the other end seemed to be heading for the safety of the mangrove roots. "Oh no you don't," I breathlessly whispered. I held my rod tip up and my line tight to prevent the fish's getaway. You have to make a decision when it feels right to start reeling in. If you begin too soon, there could be a small window of opportunity for the fish to spit out the hook, but if you wait too long, you could compromise the line in some way, allowing it to snap. By this time I could feel the fish wiggling, and I made my move.

"You got it, honey. Reel it in!" Chris yelled. I could hear him, but his voice was in the distance. I had zoned in on the fish, and that was all I could hear. I felt its strength as its bulky body tugged hard and continued to make a break for the banks, where it was sure to lose me. I held on and waited to feel its next move, anticipating, calculating, and planning what I would do. I would engage the reel only when I felt a pause from the fish, who was probably taking a breather and assessing me as well.

I felt the fish still, and I reeled in strong with a big burst of energy. Chris dipped the net and pulled up my opponent—a really big gag grouper.

"Wow!" Chris exclaimed. "This could be a keeper." We measured it quickly, and it came up two inches short. "Oh, so close," he said, disappointed.

"That's OK. Just let me take a look at it before you put it back in the water," I said. I made my way toward the bow. When I glanced down at the fish, I immediately noticed my reflection in its bulbous eyes. Its skin glistened and was in perfect combat camouflage—hues of brown and green with patterns of foliage dotting its sides and tail. "This is a magnificent fish," I said. Chris began to take the hook from its lip, and with one flick of his wrist, the massive fish fell with a plop into the rusty-colored water and was gone forever.

Our ride back to camp was quick and filled with wildlife jumping, flying, leaping, and rolling. I watched as large ospreys performed acrobatics in the sky, shaking their watered wings in midair. There were herons studying the landscape, looking for signs of food, and dolphins arching their bodies playfully. As we approached the tiny canal that leads to our dock, that old familiar tinge of apprehension surfaced: we were almost back to the dock, where—Chris had already informed me—I would be docking the boat. We slowly entered the canal and approached the weathered structure.

"OK, honey. I'll go get the truck," Chris said, and he took the giant step upward onto the wooden planks.

As Chris disappeared I noticed a handful of fishermen gathering at the fillet station, nonchalantly gazing in my direction. I cringed. *Oh no—an audience!* I thought. I did my best to ignore them, pretending I was doing something important—fiddling with the GPS and looking over our rods. As Chris came into view, I took my seat behind the throttle. My heart began to pound like a jackhammer on concrete, and my fish-smelling hand reached for the throttle. I glanced over to the road, where a pair of men in a dark-green pickup leaned over and nodded approvingly at me. *Oh God!* I thought, but my lying eyes smiled back. That one distraction was costly. I went in reverse and could not turn the boat toward Chris; I was headed back out into Chokoloskee Bay!

"Where are you going, honey? Come back this way!" Chris yelled toward me. "What are you doing?"

"Yeah, what *am* I doing?" I replied tersely under my breath. "Just shut up!" I wanted to shout. His yelling only brought more attention to me.

I kept my cool, acting as if I intended to do what I was doing. But I did not have a clue what I was doing. My inner self took control, and I noticed an area that seemed just big enough for me to turn around. Chris told me to make my correction with the wheel first, and then give it some throttle as I recalled.

"OK, honey, I'm coming. I'm just turning around!" I yelled back, just as sweetly as I could. *Correct the wheel, give some gas, and turn!* Driving a boat is a lot like trying to drive a car on a slippery slope. Even if you had brakes, they would be useless. It's all about easing yourself in position, *feeling* the boat, and making your corrections *before* giving it gas. Everything was going according to plan, as I gently turned the boat around and headed back toward Chris, who was now scratching his head and leaning on the truck for emotional support. By this time I was sitting up straight and had complete control. I had enough courage to look over to the men in the truck. They had started driving toward me, moving at the same speed.

"Hey there!" one of them yelled, "it sure is nice to see a she-captain! Wow!" I just shook my head.

After the boat was on the trailer, a fisherman came up to Chris and asked if he could hire me for a day.

"Well, she's not cheap," Chris told the man jokingly.

He looked over at me and asked directly: "How much are you? Well? Come on, *answer*—it's not a hard question." A big smile appeared across his face.

"Well…" I laughed shyly.

"She's not for hire," Chris interjected.

"Well, if you change your mind…"

"No, she is not for hire," he reiterated, laughing.

"See you later!" I said, and I jumped in the truck and turned the air on high. "Let's go, Chris! Come on!" Chris got in, and I waved in a friendly manner at the men who continued their stare.

"What the heck was that?" I asked Chris, wiping the sweat from my face.

"You sure get their attention," he answered, trying to navigate the truck through the narrow streets of our camping ground.

It's true that I haven't seen many women pulling boats up in these parts, but I'm sure there are plenty. I'm just not around when they are. For now, I'll be the novelty, no problem. I have come to know that fishermen have been nothing but encouraging toward me and go out of their way to exhibit courtesy in every endeavor.

CHAPTER 16

❖

Manatees and Music

WHEN I'M FISHING, most of my concentration converges on casting a line with precision and trying my best to stay away from all the dangling branches and sturdy roots of the mangroves that line the moistened shores of any given bank. The sounds of nature become just an obligatory distraction from my fierce fishing mind. During the moments when my line soars from its reel and drops into the water, nothing else matters. Like a quarterback about to release the game-tying ball, I zero in on my impending target. It's too late to ask the questions I should've asked myself before my throw.

"Leave it in!" Chris yelled, but I grew impatient: I wanted a bite *now*. I wanted action *now*. I am an impetuous angler, and this is not an attractive attribute.

"Whoa...whoa! Wh...what was that?" I stammered. There are very few things that will disturb a focused fisherman, but a strange sighting might do it. No gusty winds, impending rain, chatty husbands, chirping birds, or rustling leaves can scramble the signals, yet every once in a while, there will be a sound or a glimpse of something out of place—something so unique it topples your well-constructed thought process, disengaging your fishing mind from its purpose.

The large, rounded tail of a manatee was unmistakable, but what didn't make sense was its size. "Was that a *manatee*?" I asked with disbelief.

"Did you see that?" Chris asked, stepping onto the bow.

"Yeah, I did. That was a manatee, right?" I dismissed the encounter as a mere passing moment, when suddenly a large, shadowy form turned in the water and headed toward the bow of the boat. The creature had strangely returned and began to slowly surface, like an ancient artifact that had been unearthed by the river's hands. On its rotund body were patches of various shades of green and brown that looked more like patterns found on a fine paisley jacket than discoloration that had blended into its skin.

As it hovered serenely, its nostrils broke the surface, and it took a breath. *What does it want? Why is it? How? What? Why?* My questions were fragmented because I couldn't understand why it was just floating there, looking at us while we looked at it.

"It doesn't have much to say, but it seems like he'd be a good listener!" I said flippantly. After a few minutes, the manatee slowly dissolved into the depths of the turbid waters, quietly leaving us. "Wow, that was interesting," I said to Chris.

"Yep, it sure was," he replied. He extended his arms outward, walking the gunnels like a balance beam as he made his way to the stern, unfazed by this ghostlike appearance.

That was the second day of a two-day fishing trip in the Everglades National Park area and beyond. On our first day, we'd ventured out toward Houston River and scoped out various locations. We selected one of the points near a small cove, where the current whipped around a jagged bank.

I readied my stance, cast out my line, and waited. In a matter of moments, a fish answered my casting call and strongly tugged my line, causing me to stumble. The line took off with a roaring scream as the blur of monofilament sliced through the air. It was whizzing along so fast I thought I was going to get spooled. I noticed the direction of my line and realized that the fish was heading for the safety of the mangroves. *Tip up! Hold tight! Don't reel in. Just hold it!* If Chris was talking, I wasn't listening. I was in my zone, and there was nothing that could knock me off. It was me and the fish, and I was feeling pretty lucky.

My only visual was the transparent line that dragged on the surface, creating a wake that alerted me to my target area. The bulk of the work comes from understanding the muscle of your fish, and in this case it was clear to me that I had an Arnold Schwarzenegger on the other end. After a crafty attempt on the fish's part to lose me, I finally convinced it that it was coming up. As I reeled upward, the fish emerged, looking like a radiant rock with an arabesque painted on each side. Chris reached in, and as he lifted the fish with the net, its orange-red eyes peered through the moistened mesh that now held it captive.

"Wow, honey, nice fish," Chris said proudly. He worked quickly to get the hook out of the grouper's gaping mouth. I admired the fish just before it arched its body and flipped off the bow with all the finesse of a springboard champion, hitting the surface cleanly and causing just a hint of a ripple. This was quite a feat, considering its size and weight.

Houston River was now on the horizon, and we had a full high tide waiting for us. We settled on a bank near the Gulf and started our warm-up casting, using twice-frozen bait that had thawed in the empty live well. Chris encouraged me to use a treble-hooked lure, a barbaric-looking hook that has three prongs that dangle from a colorful plasticky creature that some fish find attractive. I was still trying to learn how to remove *one* hook from the gummy sides of a fish's mouth, so I declined. Besides, on this day the fish were hitting even the smallest of hooks. It wasn't long before we reached our self-imposed limit on sea trout. They were big, fat, and beautiful with their sparkly spots and golden hues. We released more than a dozen and kept three in the live well.

"Hey, honey—listen," Chris said in a whisper. "What's *that*?"

"What's what?" I asked, perplexed.

"Music!" he replied. I looked over toward the distant island and could see the fishing fete right there on Houston River, giving new meaning to *wildlife*. The sounds of clinking glass and vibrant melodies drifted from the boisterous boat, along with random celebratory screams. It all seemed rather bizarre in this normally hushed environment.

"Turn it down! You're going to scare off every fish from here to Broad River!" I exclaimed. But truth be told, I wanted to join them.

Chris and I just shook our heads and laughed it off. Soon we were pulling anchor to find a new river and some bait. Most islands are small in these parts, but big enough that you can pitch a tent or two. There are also chickees along the way that you can register to use at the ranger station in the park. I haven't tried camping on any of them, but they do seem relatively safe, with a solid structure built off the ground and a Porta Potty adjacent to the campsite. For anybody who prefers remote campsites along with fishing and exploration, these chickees would fit that bill.

The bow of our boat now rested on the shoulders of a tiny stretch of a windswept shore. Chris took his cast net, and I walked along the waterline, gazing into a sandy galaxy where starfish hovered together, forming a spectacular constellation. The cluster drifted calmly, as the current gently moved the understated creatures across their sandy sky. Chris had tried his best for bait but was coming up empty.

"There's nothing here," he said. "Let's go." I didn't mind the brief respite from the casting; my arm had a hint of fisherman's elbow, and I knew I should be taking it easy.

Our two-day trip in and around the Houston River and Chokoloskee Bay gave us an opportunity to explore new potential fishing holes, hang out with a curious manatee, tousle with an Arnold Schwarzenegger wannabe, stargaze, become an unwitting audience to a mini-Mardi Gras, and—of course—catch fish. It was about time we got out of our comfort zone.

CHAPTER 17

Lost Rod River

SITTING AT THE bar, it was abundantly clear to me that I was not going to be served a cold beverage. There were no bartenders rushing about slapping napkins in front of us, and this was no happy hour.

Our fishing day had started in earnest, and we were anxious to make our way to Lostmans River. We were all smiles as we made the curve heading into Lopez River, and then—*thunk.* Our swift-moving boat suddenly stopped, forcing me to nearly take a face-plant on the bow. *What happened?* I thought, only seconds after abruptly stopping in the middle of what appeared to be a moving river.

"Oh God," Chris said. "We hit a sandbar."

"A sandbar?" I said, perplexed.

"We've run *aground!*" Chris said angrily.

Our boat's engine had been suddenly silenced midroar by the thickness of wet, mucky mud. The only things rushing around us were the boats of passing fishermen. "This is embarrassing," I said, as we sluggishly bobbed in their wake.

"Oh well. The tide will be in, and we'll be on our way," Chris retorted flatly. "I'm marking this spot on our GPS for future reference."

Chris was still figuring out the area. This minor delay was nothing, really, although being stranded in a river is strangely surreal. This was not expected. "I'll get in and try to push us out," Chris said, and he leaped into the wintry water. I shifted my weight toward the bow, hoping to give some momentum to his push, but we didn't budge.

"OK, I'm getting out to help," I whispered, and I gently slipped into the liquid darkness. I was hoping that any stingrays that might have been sitting around on the bottom had vacated the premises with all this chaos. As my feet touched bottom, the moist mud of the riverbed grabbed my shins and began pulling me under.

"Chris, I can't seem to move! I'm stuck, and I'm sinking!" I yelled.

"What?" Chris yelled over to me, oblivious to my quagmire. He was busy looking at how the water depth looked in each direction and making his game plan, and he didn't want any further distractions coming from me.

Taking matters into my own hands, I grabbed the gunnels and somehow pulled myself out of my muddy entombment. With all my strength, I hoisted myself up and over, kicking hard all the way up and onto the deck. I sighed heavily as I began washing the mud from my legs. Meanwhile, Chris continued his quest of turning the bow this way and that until finally we started slowly moving. It had been about an hour, and the tide was charging through like wild horses just freed from their fences.

"Hey, it looks like we'll be on our way!" Chris exclaimed.

"Wahoooo!" I yelled back, trying to put the whole incident behind me. Besides, the sky was a brilliant blue, the air temperature was a cool seventy-two, and we had an incoming tide. All these things added up to what I felt was going to be a great fishing day.

As we began to drift, Chris, who was still wading in the river, yelled for me to grab the trolling motor. "You know how to use the trolling motor, *right?*" he yelled, gasping for breath.

"Yeah, I know how," I replied. I jumped up and attempted to lift the trolling motor, which was lying securely on the port side of the bow. I had never actually lifted the motor off its bracket. *How hard can it be?* I thought. I made two attempts to disengage the metal motor; neither was successful.

"Hurry, honey! The water is rising!" Chris yelled. There was a sense of urgency in his voice. *They should make these things a little more girl friendly*, I thought, trying my best to appear like I knew what I was doing.

"Aha! Got it!" I boasted. I pulled the motor up and turned it on just seconds before we reached a mangrove.

"Good job, honey! Excellent!" Chris said. Wet and exhausted, he leaped into the boat.

It appeared we would be on our way, and I was all smiles once again. But when I attempted to tug the motor up from the water, the metal bracket stiffened and kept the trolling motor from disengaging. It was now stuck in the downward position, frozen like an icicle hanging from a line.

"It won't move, Chris," I yelled. I continued to struggle with the cord that disengages the lock that keeps the motor down in the water.

"Here, let me try," Chris said. He quickly reached for the cord that dangled loosely in my hands. Chris pulled, tugged, yanked, and jerked, all to no avail. "Looks like were going back to that shallow spot," he said, clearly annoyed.

"You mean the spot we were just *freed* from?" I asked sarcastically.

"Yep, that's right. We can't go anywhere with a trolling motor stuck in the down position," he grumbled. The water was rising, and we had just a narrow window of opportunity to head back and fiddle with the motor as the last bit of the showing shoal began to disappear.

We used the trolling motor to get us back, and Chris immediately vaulted over the gunnel and started fooling around with levers, ropes, and plastic parts of the motor. "I'll call Fort Myers Marine and see if they can troubleshoot this for us," I said. I quickly dialed the number.

"Oh, hi, Colinda. How are you?" I was trying at this point to make everything seem as normal as possible. I felt kind of foolish, and I didn't want to come right out and say that Chris was up to his neck in river water and the tide was rushing in and our trolling motor was broken. It just didn't seem right. "I was wondering if Ron or one of the mechanics could talk with us. We have a slight problem," I continued. "We're kind of in a hurry."

"OK, I'll get Ron," she cheerily replied, not knowing that my husband was being swallowed by Lopez River. I handed the phone down to Chris, who did his best to dry his hand on his soaked T-shirt before grabbing it.

"Hi. Ron. Our trolling motor is stuck in the down position. Do you have any suggestions on how to fix that?" Chris spoke with a calm demeanor despite our predicament. Ron did his best to assist with the problem, while Chris swished around in the murky water. I wasn't hearing what Ron was saying, but I could tell by the conversation that they were getting somewhere.

Meanwhile, the river began to consume Chris. I couldn't help but to think of the man-eating sharks that resided in the area; I was sure they'd be delighted to have an easy meal. Chris had hung up with Ron, and I was getting anxious.

"Chris, hurry up!" I yelled. I became more frantic with the oncoming surge of the incoming tide.

"I'm going as fast as I can. I think I got it this time." He grunted as he clipped off the motor from the bracket.

"OK, get in the boat before the sharks *eat* you!" I yelled.

"Oh, stop. No shark is going to *eat* me," he replied in a mocking tone. He lifted himself up onto the boat.

Chris placed the malfunctioning motor on the deck. *Wet* and *useless* were two words that quickly came to mind as I looked it over. "Well, we can't fish today, not with this on board," he flatly said.

"Oh heck no—we are going fishing!" I sternly yelled with a furrowed brow. "We'll just step over it," I insisted. "After all of *this* and not go fishing? I don't think so!"

Chris did not argue with me. "OK, honey. We'll go fishing," he said in a melodic tone, and he readied the boat for departure. We were once again off to our destination, roaring toward the south. We were a little wet and frustrated, but determined nonetheless.

I sat on the edge of my seat, with my foot firmly bracing against the console, just in case of any more sudden stops. Chris laughed it off and remained confident in his navigational skills despite the fact that he was still getting reacquainted with the area. Just because you have a GPS on board doesn't mean that you should blindly believe in it. There are many changes that occur that a navigational tool does not pick up, such as the ever-changing soggy bottom. The GPS is a good thing to have, but honestly, it's overrated. The best thing to do is to familiarize yourself the old-fashioned way—with map reading and gaining an understanding of the area you'll be fishing *before* leaving the dock.

Chris was now hitting his stride and soaring through the emerald-green waterway. The winds were refreshing, and we both had a renewed interest in the day's fishing expedition. Our plan was to cruise into Lostmans River and anchor down on an incoming tide that would provide us with a new batch of scaly treasure along the jagged landscape.

"Hey, look—there's fish on TV!" Chris lightheartedly quipped. He pointed toward the fish finder. I find it humorous to watch the finder, which is incorporated into the GPS system. When you push a certain button, it displays fish leisurely swimming below. The image on the screen looks more like a child's toy aquarium, where fish continually swim by. *What an* ingenious *marketing concept*, I thought with a hint of sarcasm. On our screen the fish were the color of gold and came in various sizes. "There sure are a lot of them!" Chris exclaimed as the computerized fish silently continued swimming. The screen might indicate fish, but it doesn't tell what kind of fish they are. When that happens, I will be *really* impressed.

We settled, finally, and the sounds of hunting osprey pierced the morning air. I gazed upward and watched as the stealthy hunters dipped their talons in the water and flew away with their fishy prize. "Wow! Now *that's* precision," I said, marveling at the feathery fishermen. By then I had become slightly distracted, something that doesn't bode well for anglers. Your concentration has to be on the task at hand, or you will miss that ever-so-slight tug on the end of your line.

"You should tighten your line, honey," Chris said, looking toward my cast.

"OK, I'm trying, but the tide must be changing because when I throw over there, my line ends up here," I said. I gestured toward the left.

After a few tactical changes, we were pulling in sheepshead and black drum. Our conversation was all over the map, from music and other incidental topics to what we were going to have for dinner that night. We laughed and argued about this and that while still managing to hook a few keeper-sized snapper. As we continued baiting and bantering, the bite eventually slowed, and we pulled anchor and headed to our next favorite spot. We had determined that the tide was indeed going out and anticipated some good fishing.

"Chris, it's going to be tough to anchor here," I said with some reservation. The water was ripping by as it headed out toward the Gulf. The pace quickened, and anything that had been stilled by the slack tide had awakened and was being ushered out into the open sea. I tossed our small anchor into the fury and laughed as it seemed to run back to the boat in fear. "I've got to throw it again—it's not catching!" I yelled back to Chris.

I knelt precariously on the bow. I decided to throw it closer to the bank, hoping it would find ground. Growing tired from the strenuous task, I decided to sit down by the gunnel. When I tossed the anchor up and forward, it hit the boat, chipped off part of the gunnel, and got stuck on the side of the boat. Perplexed by this dilemma, I reached for the anchor's metal prong, lost my footing, and kicked my rod, which was leaning against the gunnel. To my horror, I watched it teeter slowly and fall into the rapid river and disappear.

"My rod!" I screamed. I did my best to reach into the water, but I could only grab water. I stopped short of jumping in after it—I knew that would be a fool's errand.

Everything stilled. I could hear nothing. I was paralyzed by the vision and could do nothing about it. The rod was gone. We were now in a sweet fishing spot, and my lucky rod was gone. "Honey, you shouldn't leave your pole lying around," Chris said as gently as he could. I just glared at him. I thought it was best to say nothing, because what I wanted to say was not very nice, to put it mildly.

I sat alone in my stupor, accompanied only by the merciless mosquitoes. To say that I was sulking would be an understatement. I was having a full-blown pity party. I looked skyward and told God that I wasn't even going to ask him to bring back my rod: "OK, God, it's gone. I know," I muttered, looking into the depths of Lostmans River as it continued its retreat toward the Gulf of Mexico with my prized rod. Meanwhile, Chris kept reeling them in.

"Hey, I got a big one! Hurry—get the net!" he yelled toward me. His biceps bulged. I leaped up, forgetting all about my problems as the adrenaline started pumping. I'm not one to wallow in my misfortunes: what's done is done.

Chris's rod was now arching toward the water, indicating that a heavy fish was on the other end. "Can you see it yet?" I asked with excitement.

"It's a sheepshead, a really big one!" Chris yelled. I lunged forward and dropped to my knees in anticipation of the fish that was now ready for me to scoop it up with the net. I lifted the sheepshead out as it continued its struggle. "Wow, this is probably the biggest sheepshead I've ever caught!" he exclaimed proudly. He reached into the net and hoisted his prize. The heavy fish continued its fight, proving its prowess and not giving in. "Hold the net while I get the hook out," Chris said, and he began the process of releasing the metal object that jutted out from the fish's gum. The giant fish watched his every move, and in its eyes I could see defeat.

After Chris's big catch, we sat silently, looking out on the horizon as the afternoon clouds started forming over the Gulf. I was still in my feel-sorry-for-myself mode, but I continued to brush it off. *I can't get it back*, I told myself. *Get over it.* I was troubled by my behavior and tried hard to put on a happy face.

"Well, I think it's time to go," Chris said, lifting himself off his chair, "I'll pull anchor."

"Good, because I don't want to," I replied flatly. Chris knelt on the bow and began the process of pulling up the moistened rope.

"Wow, this thing's really stuck," he groaned, yanking at the taught line. He steadied his stance, and with a strong tug to his right, the anchor gave way. Chris started to laugh as he pulled in the rope.

"What? What's so funny?" I asked.

"Well, what do we have here?" he said. "A hook and a swivel!" He pulled faster, and as he pulled, a strange shape appeared from the depths of the river. It was my rod, and it was attached to the anchor rope! I was stunned! I grabbed the wet rod, which was still dripping with some mud, hoisted it in the air, and did the happy dance, nearly capsizing the boat.

"Here, pour some fresh water on your reel," Chris yelled. "We have to get the salt off quickly." I doused the cherry-red Penn reel with cool freshwater, treating it more like a beloved pet than a fishing reel.

The ride back to Chokoloskee was exhilarating in many ways: I had my prized rod back, and Chris had caught a prized fish. The bay stretched out before us like a welcoming friend, and Chris popped open a cold beer as we approached. He sipped on his beer as I sang songs off-key while we went whizzing through the water. I glanced at the port side to see if there were any other boats heading toward the ramp, and I saw a large grayish boat flying toward us like an F-16 fighter jet.

"What the hell?" I yelled. At first it didn't register that it was law enforcement. It all seemed so random. One minute we were sailing along, happy and free, and the next we were being hunted down by uniformed water rangers! Buzzkill!

I sat stoically as rangers in new-looking uniforms stood a short distance from the gunnels of their boat with their binoculars fastened to their faces. This jarring reality was at first scary, but once I calmed down, I knew that we had nothing to worry about. It was just their approach that seemed so unnecessary. Unlike land officers, water officers can pull you over for no reason. It's their job to stop boaters, no matter how innocent they may appear, and I'm OK with that.

"Get out your license and registration please," the officer said sternly. He attempted to tie his boat to ours. "Sir, can you please tie the rope to your boat?" Chris got up and stumbled toward the back of the boat, not because he was intoxicated but because the wake from their boat was large due to the rate of speed they approached us with. After several attempts, Chris roped off their boat successfully. The officer continued: "I'll need to see all of your regulation gear, and I'll need for you to open all hatches and your trash cans. I'll also need to measure all your fish," he said matter-of-factly, and he boarded our boat.

As the ranger lifted the hatch to our live well, the fish went wild, especially that giant sheepshead, whose dorsal fin was straight-up ready to pierce his law enforcement fingers! "If they jump out, sir, that's OK," Chris said, seeing the officer struggle with our catch.

"Heck no!" I yelled angrily. "Officer, please don't lose our fish. It took us *all* day to catch them. I'll help you! Besides, you don't know what we've been through!"

After we'd provided all the necessary emergency equipment, the officer instructed us to sit on the bow while he measured our fish. "Watch these two," he said to his partner. "Keep your eye on them." Chris and I looked at each other, and I tried to contain myself as laughter bubbled up in my mouth. As I walked toward the bow, I noticed Chris's open container, and I was really hoping the officers *hadn't*. It didn't matter anyway, really; this was the second beer Chris had consumed, and I was as sober as a Sunday preacher.

"OK, your fish are legal," he said. He stepped over our gunnels and boarded his boat. *Oh yay, he didn't mention the open container!* I thought. I smiled toward the pair, and just as I was taking my seat, the officer said, "Oh, there's just one more thing." *Uh-oh, here it comes.* "There's an open container of alcohol, and, sir, you appear impaired."

Chris was not having any of that. "I am not impaired. I'm just enjoying a beer on the way back to the ramp," he stated with manly confidence.

"Well, you weren't following my orders, and you were stumbling."

"I wasn't stumbling. I just couldn't hear you, and the water's wake was tossing the boat around." By now I was getting frustrated. Chris *never* drinks excessively on a fishing trip.

"Officer, I'm driving, and I know how to handle the boat," I stated firmly. "I haven't had any alcohol today." The ranger stood with his arms crossed and looked in my direction.

His faced softened slightly. "Oh, OK," he said. "I'm not opposed to someone having fun. We just want you to be responsible."

"We understand, officer," Chris interjected.

"Well, OK, you two are free to go," he said. He and his partner prepared to depart. That was music to my sunburned ears! I took control of the throttle and pushed it forward, as if I was popping a wheelie.

"Well, isn't that the way this day should end!" I yelled. The water churned wildly under the boat.

"Now go easy on the throttle, honey," Chris said. Some beer spilled from his can. "Try not to be so jerky!"

"OK," I said, laughing. I was really happy to see the small canal in front of me. It had been quite a day, and I was hoping that nothing else would happen. I crept along the small waterway and slowed to drop Chris off at the dock. After a few minutes, he appeared with the truck.

"Let's get out of here," I said wearily.

"Yeah, let's," Chris said in agreement, and the sound of dripping water and roaring engines echoed in the fading afternoon light.

CHAPTER 18

Reel Salty

WHILE WRESTLING WITH my salt-corroded, stuck-in-its-position, gear-crunching reel, it suddenly occurred to me that I should ask Chris to buy me a new one. This would be a difficult request, considering I was the one who had been negligent in gently giving my prized rod and reel a kick overboard. I still had flashbacks of the incident; the scenario could not be purged from my memory, no matter how hard I tried. It was the same each time: the long, thin, glittery blue rod with the apple-red reel slowly going over and disappearing into the raging waters of Lostmans River, the look of disbelief on Chris's face. It was rather clumsy of me, and I had since been more careful with my fishing gear, but that did not solve my issue regarding my reel: using it now felt more like trying to wind thick mud through the eye of a needle. I had to really give an Academy Award–winning performance to give Chris the idea that all was right with my reel. I was just not up for the I-told-you-so speech that was sure to follow once he learned that the reel was *not* all right. I resigned myself to doing my best with the crusty reel for the time being.

Our first stop on this frigid fishing day was just outside of Lopez River. Our location seemed to be the perfect area to catch something. It had an out-going tide, a deep hole, and a point that had large roots sticking out where the fast current crossed over, creating a wild rippling effect on the surface of the frosty water. I sized up the situation as I stood on the bow, tossed my line at the swift current, and counted to ten before flipping my bail. I wanted to be sure my bait sank to the bottom. I've learned that you have to wait for the bait to sink. If you flip your bail too early, your bait floats around just under the surface, and that usually doesn't generate interest. Sometimes it does, but I get more bites if the bait goes down to the bottom.

A few minutes had passed, and just as I began trying my best to wrestle with my rod, I managed to hook a speckled trout and reel it in. "Oh, hey, he's a keeper," Chris gleefully yelled, and he threw another cast into the water.

"Oh, I don't know," I cautiously whispered. I inspected my catch as its wet flesh glistened in the morning sun. I have discovered that speckled trout are quite demure. They don't flop around, and they generally don't give you any fight after you hoist them on board. They also are one of the few fish that die really quickly if you don't get them back in the water, so I stepped it up, grabbing the pink rag off the console and walking the fish to the measuring stick. I had to be certain that the fish was slot size, and much to my surprise, it came up short. The fish now seemed overly still: its mouth was frozen in midbreath, as if it was gasping and in midbreath and then died. "Oh no! No fish, don't die!" I said. I quickly released the hook from its gaping mouth. I placed the fish in the water, and to my astonishment it swished its tail—feebly at first and then with much fervor—and took off into the murky water.

"Thank goodness!" I yelled with a sense of relief. "It survived!"

After a few more casts that came up empty, we pulled anchor and headed south. We traveled across a few bays and slowed the boat to idle, creeping along through the winding waters of Alligator Creek. Above us the sky resembled a picture-perfect Florida postcard, with its vibrant shades of blue dotted with marshmallow-sized clouds that seemed to be suspended in time. Gentle-looking pelicans flew along on the distant horizon. I had to remind myself that as lovely and serene as the creek felt, there were gators lurking in the shadows.

As we twisted our way through the blood-colored water, I caught a glimpse of aquatic eyes that appeared just above the shoreline, staring in my direction. The creature was slowly swishing and easing into what appeared to be a defense posture while observing our every move. I wasn't afraid, but I was still relieved that I was in a boat. As we slowly idled on, I began to think about our sixteen-foot boat. Doing the math in my head, I realized that a ten-foot gator would need only six feet more to equal the size of our boat. In addition, our boat is really lightweight. Math gets really simple when you have a feeling your life may be in peril.

I was near giddy by the time we reached the creek's mouth, which opens up into Alligator Bay—partly because we had left the creek's namesake behind us and partly because we were nearing our destination. As Chris pushed the throttle forward, I clutched my coat tightly around the neck and braced myself for the wintery wind. I thought I had prepared for the chill by wearing layer on top of layer, but somehow the crisp air found its way through the seams of my defense. I regretted my suggestion to go to Lostmans River, which was about an hour ride from Chokoloskee Island.

After enduring a frigid ride, we slowed the boat into the river, where we prepared to cast a few lines. I sat on the gunnels with my teeth chattering, struggling with a rod that had endured a near-death experience. It wasn't operating as it once had, and the throw I attempted was far from stealthy. I still have confidence in my rod—I have to. It's an Outlaw rod, and Outlaws are true fighters (well, at least mine is). Besides, we had made it to Lostmans River, and what better place for an outlaw to be? Such were the thoughts that were running through my head as I tried to convince myself that I was not having issues. Chris and I had earlier talked about going to West Pass, but he agreed to take me to Lostmans. The river had been my go-to place recently, like a favorite restaurant. I wanted to go there every chance I had. Fishing can be great in that area, and I wanted nothing less than great fishing. But it was cold, and everything looked cold. The water, the sky, the landscape—it just had that cold look and feel to it that always strikes me as odd, since it's usually warm when we visit.

"Let's go over there." I gestured to a familiar fishing hole, and Chris gingerly navigated the boat over the treacherously shallow waters. Now it became abundantly clear why no other boaters were headed over in our direction: it was so shallow you could nearly count every grain of sand on the bottom. Chris calls it skinny water; I call it crazy water. You practically have to get out and carry your boat over to the banks in these conditions. They don't call them flats boats for nothing—you really need one during low tide in Lostmans River. You also need a good trolling motor. These come in real handy when it's too shallow for your outboard. Chris is always making sure that we aren't kicking up mud, and we try our best not to cause harm to the important nutrients that thrive in the shallows of the river.

After expertly navigating over to the bank, we put down our shallow-water anchor and baited our hooks. Somehow I wasn't feeling the same that day as I had on other fishing days out there. Maybe it was the cold, or maybe I was starting to realize I should have gone with Chris's suggestion and gone to West Pass. I was certain the fishing would be just as slow there, since it would be just as cold. After a few casts toward the bank, I shifted my stance toward the bow. I adjusted my scarf and, in doing so, jiggled my earring loose. The earring teetered for a brief moment, and, as if in slow motion, it fell into the inky waters with a soft plunk.

"My earring!" I shouted with disappointment.

"Why do you wear earrings out here anyway? It's stupid," Chris said, laughing.

"Well, because I *want* to wear earrings, OK?" I replied, a bit of antagonism in my tone.

Oh well, I thought. I took the other earring out and put it in my pocket as I headed to the live well for another shrimp. After baiting my hook, I backhanded it toward the banks. For some reason I am way better at a backhanded casting. In fact, I'm better at navigating the boat out of a jam by thrusting it in reverse as well. Chris is always cajoling me to just ease into forward, make a wide loop, and then come back to the targeted area if we overshoot a fishing hole. But I prefer to back out of it and navigate that way, and I'm not sure why I am the way I am. This would probably be something for the fishing gurus to unravel, but for now I'll just say it works for me.

I had loosened up my reel, and that sent my line soaring toward the bank. It wasn't long before I got a nice tug and set the hook. Chris is always telling me to set the hook if I want to reel one in, but I'm still trying to figure that technique out. When I feel a tug, I pull my rod up and away, and somehow that works for me. Maybe I'm setting the hook and just don't know it. It's all about the feel with me, and most of the time, it works.

As I reeled in, I could see the shiny, silvery body of a sheepshead. These fish are feisty fighters; they have no mercy at all if you happen to bring them on board and have the audacity to go near their mouths to unhook them. But you should consider yourself lucky if you can even hook one of these backcountry bandits. They can swiftly steal your bait with cunning precision, and you won't even know it. Several years of fishing had passed before I learned the fine art of hooking a sheepshead, and it has taken me just as long to even begin to come close to this fish once it's hoisted on board. They throw hellacious tantrums and look at you as if they will inflict bodily harm if you even dare to come close. This, of course, is an effective scare tactic to a novice like me. To Chris, a sheepshead is just like any other fish. He'll grab it from underneath, measure it, and—if it's not legal—toss it back in without a care in the world.

I approached my fish with mild trepidation this time. I had found some bravery in myself recently, and I gingerly bent down toward the sheepshead, which was now staring me down and whacking its tail against the deck.

"OK, fish," I calmly said, and with a swift scoop from underneath, I won out over its tussling. The hook was a different matter. After several failed attempts to navigate through the oddly human-looking teeth, I just couldn't get the hook out. I yelled for Chris, who set his rod down and agreed to help me.

"Well, here's your problem," he said, pointing out that the hook had lodged through the fish's face and circled back in. It appeared that I had given the fish a new nostril, and I wasn't happy about it. "He'll be OK," Chris said with great assurance. "Now watch how I do this." He used his pliers to bend the hook straight and gently guided the hook through the fish's battleship-gray face. There was no blood, but the fish seemed stunned by the whole incident. Its coloring had begun to dull, indicating that death was near. "OK, let's get him back in the water," Chris said, and he gently submerged the limp fish into the water while moving it around, gently forcing water into its gills. Suddenly the fish began to stir and appeared as if it were waking up from a bad dream. It wiggled, thrashed, and flipped its tail in my direction before it disappeared.

We made some attempts to fish other favorite spots, but the water had stirred up so much, it looked as if we were gliding along on the top of a big cup of café au lait. "Let's head back home," I said with a tinge of disappointment.

"OK, I'm ready," Chris said.

The wind showed us the way out of the mouth of the river and into Lostmans Second Bay. The air was still crisp, even as the afternoon sun coated the horizon with a swath of glittering gold accents along the shoreline, as if an artist had just finished her final touches. I was taken aback by the sense of warmth despite the temperature, and I entertained myself by admiring the light on the surface of the water that twinkled like the diamonds on Liberace's lapel.

As we turned and made our way into Plate Creek Bay, I was suddenly shaken out of my daydream by an unexpected pod of playful dolphins that made a point to soar into the air just in front of the bow. "Oh my gosh!" I yelled over the roar of the engine. I glanced back toward Chris from my cooler seat in the front. He nodded as if he knew what I was yelling about and slowed the boat. The dolphin made another appearance and flipped its tail toward my direction, dousing me in a spray of refreshing water.

"Oh, thank you," I said to the dolphin. "I needed to pay closer attention to where we're going anyway." I laughed, and Chris continued on. If there's one thing I have learned out in the wild, it's that you have to pay attention, no matter how intoxicating your surroundings are. Things can happen quickly. Just ask the local Plate Creek Bay dolphins—they can explain it all in one flip of their tail.

CHAPTER 19

The NauticStar

"Chris, this is *spooky*," I whispered. We had idled into a shadowy cove near Broad River. The atmosphere was hushed except for an aberrant breeze that hissed through the branches of spooky-looking trees with leafless branches draped in decay.

"This could be good," Chris replied, unfazed by the fact that it appeared as if we were floating in the stew of a witch's cauldron. The waters were shallow and disturbed, making navigation difficult.

"Let's go around that corner and see what's there," he said. He motioned toward some dense shrubbery. We hit a dead end, but I noticed that there was an entryway big enough for fish to swim in and out of. "I think this is perfect," Chris said, marveling at his discovery. "We have structure, a slight current, and it just *feels* right." I glanced around. The only thing I felt was trapped.

Chris lowered the shallow anchor and noticed a bizarre branch that tapped oddly at the water's surface. "Hey, that branch is telling me to throw my line over there," he said, laughing.

"Yeah, sure," I replied sarcastically. I was trying to plan my escape route from this fearsome place. He casually tossed his line toward the twisted branch and got an instant bite.

"Hey, the branch was right—I got a nice fish on the line," he yelled excitedly. I was shocked but not surprised, considering we were surrounded by paranormal forces. "Get the net ready!" Chris instructed.

In a flash a large, dark object surfaced and raced toward Chris's line. "It's a *shark*! Its going for my fish!" he yelled, reeling faster to try to get his catch on board. Just as he lifted the fish in the air, the bull shark lunged, barely missing us. Its tail swished hard, causing instability in the boat. "Whoa, that was crazy!" Chris said. I picked up my rod, enflamed by this occurrence, and swung at the water as if it were a birthday piñata.

"Scram, shark! Scram!" I yelled. My fear had morphed into annoyance, and once I tired of my nonsense, I realized that I really should be careful. "Please, let's go," I urged Chris." I don't like this place." Chris agreed to go and lifted the anchor, still laughing about the shark incident.

On the next day of fishing, Chris decided to go south, toward Houston River, where I welcomed the fresh perspective of the luminous landscape. I'd gotten to know the area pretty well, and I started pointing out areas where snook might be hanging out. After anchoring, I made a few casts and got a snag that snapped my line. Frustrated, I sat down hard on the cooler to begin the task of rigging. My fingers lack deftness, and I spend more time fumbling than fishing sometimes. Chris no longer helps me, unless I ask, and even then he seems somewhat irritated while tying my leader line on. I had no time to wipe off the dried sea salt that had somehow covered my eyeglasses; I just wanted to hurry up and start fishing again. I placed the weight on and tried to tie the swivel, but I missed the loop that I was supposed to thread the end of the line through. Ugh, tying rigs can be as tedious as trying to glue tiny model-airplane parts together. Anyway, this was mostly a catch-and-release day, so I tried to go easy on myself.

We scouted around some more and discovered a place where the tide threatened to dissolve the banks it was slicing across.

"Hey Chris, there's current and a point. Let's try over there," I said, gesturing to the west. The Gulf of Mexico was visible in the distance, making this area a good choice for fish on the move. We had enough shrimp left to make it a worthwhile spot, so we anchored up. I took one side of the stern and Chris took the other, and in unison we cast out into the waters, where the sunlight on the water looked like sparks flying off a welder's cutting torch. The current was thick with snapper, making this an area to remember, and the bottom *seemed* to be free of snags—except when it was time to pull anchor.

After several attempts at tugging, I had to ask Chris for help with the heavy metal hook. He took the rope, and I took the wheel. "Turn when I tell you," he shouted. I gave it gas and moved to the right and then gave it more gas and turned to the left. "This thing is stuck," Chris scoffed.

I tried my best to reverse and go forward and make wide turns, attempting to dislodge the anchor, but nothing worked. By this time the sun had fallen deeper into the western horizon, and I felt nervous. "Let's try one more time, and if this doesn't work, we'll have to cut it free," Chris said. I could hear the disappointment in his voice. "Go ahead—start up the engine." I turned the key, and nothing happened.

"It won't start," I yelled, frustrated by our predicament. Chris scurried over from the bow and turned the key again. Nothing.

"Uh-oh," he said suspiciously.

"Uh-oh *what*?" I demanded. Chris nonchalantly went back to the bow to inspect the engine.

"Damn!" he groaned.

"What?"

"Tilt the engine up," he yelled toward me from the stern. As the engine revealed itself, so did the problem: our anchor rope had somehow wound itself around the propeller. *Great*, I thought, *our propeller is being strangled by our anchor rope!*

"I can get this," I said calmly. I knelt on the stern, stretched my arm, and grabbed the wet rope. Meanwhile, the wind began whipping, and the boat jostled me about with every gust. I tried to unwind the scratchy, braided brown fiber from the prop, but I couldn't quite loop it over high enough. Glancing into the distance, I noticed that, in all the commotion, our flotation cushion had fallen from the boat and was now headed out to open seas.

"Let's not worry about that," Chris said. "I'll give this a try."

Even with his long arms, we couldn't get it unraveled. After pausing for a moment, we came up with a new tactic: Chris would lie on the stern, hanging over, while I sat on top of his legs to keep him from falling in. This had to work!

"Now don't get up, whatever you do," Chris said. He placed himself down. I sat on his legs, and he reached over.

"Got it!" he yelled. I nearly stood up in excitement but thankfully remembered to stay put. We made one more attempt at pulling the anchor, and we were successful. "Let's go get our cushion and get back to camp," Chris said. I could tell he was relieved that our drama had been short-lived. "We've got to get this boat ready to take to Fort Myers Marine."

Our Hewes Redfisher was a tough boat. She had withstood the choppy waves of the Gulf of Mexico, the mighty forces of a shark on the hunt, and the salty tears of the sea swiping against her gunnels. Her attributes were many and complaints few, but it was the lack of space that did her in. There was no room for our growing family, who wanted to venture out with us. After much discussion, we'd decided to trade her in.

"Did we get everything out?" Chris asked.

"Yep, all done," I replied. We made the trek toward Fort Myers Marine, where I'm sure they must think that we trade boats quicker than partners at a country square dance.

Our new nineteen-foot NauticStar seemed to be levitating in the darkened garage while busy men scurried by, not noticing her supernatural stunt.

"There it is," Chris beamed. We went through our tutorial quickly and readied the boat for the trip home. The staff at Fort Myers Marine had made good on their promise to get our boat delivered before my brother Jim arrived from New York, and I couldn't have been happier. It was important to me that his first experience in the Ten Thousand Islands was a good one, and having a spacious boat that could accommodate big guys, a full cooler, rods and reels, tackle, and one fishergirl would certainly help.

Our NauticStar performed well through the high winds that threatened to smash us into the shores off Cape Romano and endured the heavy rains that were trying to persuade us to turn back. We stayed put and fished on. Rain and winds couldn't pull us from our hole, because I was bound and determined for my brother to hook a red. Cast after cast was coming up short, and as the final muted rays of sunlight started to fade, so did the hope of hooking that one keeper red.

"It's OK," Jim said. "But before we go, can you take a picture of me fishing here with the mangroves in the background?"

"Sure," I replied. "I just have to wipe the rain drops from the lens." I clamored up onto the bow as the rain continued to trickle down from the sky, and through the moistened viewfinder, I saw Jim shift from a casual stance to a serious posture.

"I got one!" he yelled, and the fight was on. With the Ten Thousand Islands serving as the perfect backdrop, he hooked a big red and brought it aboard.

A few weeks later, after Jim had left, Chris reminded me that we had about five hours left toward our twenty-hour service: "We have to take the boat out. We can rack up hours if we go south!" We loaded the boat and made our way to Chokoloskee for some light tackle fishing.

"Let's anchor up at our supersecret spot," Chris said, pushing the throttle forward. As we neared the densely covered cove, I sprayed a mist of bug spray, anticipating the heavy onslaught of biting bugs. Chris lowered the power pole down, and I baited up and eyed the banks. I noticed a tree that held some promise, and I cast in its direction. I nestled my pole into my lucky spot (on the right side of my abdomen) and waited, expecting nothing. And then *everything* happened.

A big fish was now on my line, and my pole sank deep into my gut. "Chris, it's big! Get the net," I called out. This time I held strong as the fish squirmed and fought hard. I watched its monofilament captor tighten its grip, and I kept an eye on its direction, never allowing the fish to get to the banks. Its cunning maneuvers and smart tactics were useless. I had this one, and I knew it. Strong lines and steady stamina had replaced the frayed lines and jerky motions of the past.

"It's ready," I said confidently. Chris knelt down and scooped the heavy grouper up onto the deck, where its eyes met mine. This time my reflection was clear, and I felt honored to be near the water warrior that watched my every move.

"Wow! Nice fish!" Chris exclaimed.

"Yeah, how about that!" I said, grabbing my pink rag. I gently lifted the fish as best as I could, considering its massive girth, posed for a photo, and then released it back into the honey-colored waters of West Pass. Now *that's* fishing like a girl!

Author Bio

JUDY WESTON HAS spent most of her life peering through the lens of a Nikon camera covering both international and local news for various organizations before trading in her camera for a fishing pole. This landlubber turned surf-n-turfer happily resides in Southwest Florida where she spends time searching for the next bona fide fishing spot while relishing in the carefree life of a born-again Parrothead.

Fisherman's Prayer

God, grant that I may live to fish
Until my dying day,
And when it comes to my last cast
I then most humbly pray,
When in the Lord's safe landing net
I'm peacefully asleep,
That in his mercy I be judged
As big enough to keep.
AMEN

Made in the USA
San Bernardino, CA
07 March 2017